MISS ADAMS WILL BE WAITING

A Play

ARTHUR LOVEGROVE

SAMUEL   FRENCH

LONDON

NEW YORK   TORONTO   SYDNEY   HOLLYWOOD

© 1978 BY ARTHUR LOVEGROVE

ISBN 0 573 11280 0

MISS ADAMS WILL BE WAITING

First produced at the Theatre Royal, Windsor, on February 2nd, 1971, with the following cast of characters:

Kay	Dinah Sheridan
John	Moray Watson
Mavis	Dorothy Primrose
Delivery Boy	Cyril Gates
A Visitor	William Dexter

The play directed by Joan Riley

Subsequently produced at the Yvonne Arnaud Theatre, Guildford, on March 25th, 1975, followed by a tour presented by Triumph Theatre Productions Ltd, with the following cast of characters:

Kay	Moira Lister
John	Richard Todd
Mavis	Diane Hart
Delivery Boy	Christopher Edmunds
A Visitor	Terence Longdon

The play directed by Jan Butlin

The action of the play takes place in Kay Brent's flat in a Kensington square

ACT I SCENE 1 Spring
      SCENE 2 Summer

ACT II SCENE 1 Autumn
      SCENE 2 Winter

Time — the present

ACT I

SCENE 1

Kay Brent's flat in a Kensington Square. A spring afternoon

The scene is a lounge-cum-dining-room. A large couch and two armchairs face the fireplace in the "fourth wall". A small table to one side of the couch holds a telephone and a large vase full of a gay selection of spring flowers. Four doors lead off the room: to the landing, the bedroom, the bathroom; and to the kitchenette, very small and modern—which is seen. Large studio windows look out on to a Kensington square. As the flat is four floors up, only the tops of the houses opposite, a few buildings behind them, and the open sky, are visible. The whole scene is tastefully furnished, gay but not extravagant, showing that Kay is a woman of taste. (See plan of set on p. 55)

When the CURTAIN *rises the stage is empty, and bright with the sunlight of a spring afternoon. After a moment, voices off are heard outside the landing door*

Kay (*off*) Careful, the landing is rather small.
John (*off*) That's all right, I can manage.
Kay (*off*) If you can also manage to take this parcel I'll be able to get my keys out of my handbag . . . Thank you.

There is the sound of a key in the lock then the front door opens and Kay enters, loaded with parcels. She is a very attractive woman, in her very early forties. Gay, humorous, and forthright

Thank heaven the lift was working. Usually some idiot leaves the gate open and I have to climb up four floors. (*She crosses to the couch and drops her parcels on it, and peels off her gloves*)

Meanwhile John, also loaded with parcels, stands hesitantly in the doorway. He is an ordinary-looking man of about fifty. Kindly, a trifle shy, and sometimes a little pompous. His sober dress and bowler hat betokens "something in the City"

(*Busily*) I really don't know what I'd have done if you hadn't come along, Sir Galahad.
John (*still hovering in the doorway*) I'm not really. He wore shining armour. I don't think Guinevere would have exactly gone for a bowler hat.
Kay (*turning*) Oh, I'm terribly sorry, do please come in. Drop that lot on the couch.

John Thank you. (*He nudges the door to close it, then moves to the couch*) He had a prancing steed too! (*He drops the parcels on the couch*)

Kay Not very suitable for people loaded with parcels. Your taxi was far more useful. You don't have to wear shining armour and ride a prancing steed to rescue damsels in distress.

John (*now relieved of parcels, hastily removing his hat and revealing a thick head of hair going silver at the temples*) It would look very effective.

Kay Not down the Brompton Road.

John Parking would present problems.

Kay That's a thought. Can you hitch a prancing steed to a parking-meter?

John I don't know, but if you did I doubt whether you would find it towed away.

They laugh

Kay I wonder how much they would charge if they did?

John The police? Probably a bit more than a pony.

Kay A pony?

John (*patiently*) A pony is racing slang for twenty-five pounds.

Kay Oh? (*She suddenly laughs*) I see!

A brief pause

John Well, I'd better go. I am delighted to have been of service to you.

He moves to the door

Kay Don't go!

John stops

I mean, stay and have a cup of tea. It's the least I can do.

John Well . . .

Kay Are you in a hurry?

John (*definitely*) No!

Kay That's settled then. Take off your coat and I'll put the kettle on.

Kay goes into the kitchenette, fills the kettle, lights the stove, and puts the kettle on to boil. Meanwhile, John removes his overcoat. He looks around not quite knowing where to put it. Eventually he lays it on the window-seat and places his hat carefully on top of it, and then looks out of the window. Kay puts cups and saucers on a tray, adds milk and sugar, and starts to put tea in the pot

How do you like your tea?

John Oh, as it comes.

Kay Well, actually it comes in tea-bags.

John Well, I like it strong.

Kay Strong it will be. (*She enters the lounge*) Do you like my view?

John A Kensington square! It's lovely.

Kay (*kneeling on the window seat*) I love it. (*Pointing*) See that tree, the big one?

John Yes.

Kay My tree.

John Yours?

Kay Mine, only don't tell the Council, they don't know it.

John I promise.

Kay You aren't on the Council, are you?

John No.

Kay That's all right then. I use the gardens a lot, they're so peaceful. In the summer I take my deck-chair out there and sit under my tree.

John A beech.

Kay And the one next to it?

John A sycamore.

Kay I say, you are clever.

John A legacy from the Boy Scouts, my nature badge. I can tie knots, too.

Kay You must be indispensable about the house. (*She rises*) I'll get rid of my hat and coat.

She goes into the bedroom, leaving the door open

John (*still looking out of the window*) Whenever I see a Kensington square I go all *Greenery Street* and Christopher Robin, if you know what I mean. My God! That dates me. You wouldn't know what I mean.

Kay appears in the doorway

Kay Why not? I adored *Greenery Street* but nobody reads Denis Mackail nowadays.

John I suppose not. He wrote about nice people.

Kay *The Young Livingstones*!

John I say, have you read that?

Kay Years ago! I'd love to read it again. I lost my copy and I believe it's out of print now.

John I've got one. I'd love to lend it to you. Fancy meeting someone who has read Denis Mackail.

Kay That dates me, too.

John (*gallantly*) I'm sure the copy you had was very second-hand.

Kay (*with a mock curtsy*) Thank you, you really are Sir Galahad, but it was a new copy.

John It ran into several editions.

Pause. The kettle whistles

Kay Ah! tea in a moment.

Kay rushes into the kitchenette. John turns and looks around the room, then goes to the coffee-table and picks up a magazine. Kay, meanwhile, pours hot water into the tea-pot which she puts on the tray. She takes a large cake-tin from the shelf

Do you like seed cake, home made?

John Love it.

Kay Good. (*She opens the tin*) Hell! There's only sultana.

John I love that, too.

Kay (*popping her head out of the kitchenette*) You really are most accommodating. What cake don't you like?

John Any fruit cake with cherries in it.

Kay Me too! They set my teeth on edge. (*She pops back into the kitchenette again and puts the cake on the plate*)

John We seem to have a lot in common.

Kay Soul mates! Think what a beautiful life we could lead together. (*She again pops her head through the doorway*) Reading Denis Mackail and eating seed cake.

John Or sultana.

Kay But anything with cherries in it . . .

John Definitely not.

Kay Definitely! Can you be an angel and get rid of those parcels from the couch?

John Certainly, but where do they go from there?

Kay Anywhere, there's plenty of floor space.

Kay again goes back into the kitchenette. John starts to collect the parcels, hesitates for a moment, then decides to put them on an armchair

John What are they?

Kay What are what?

John These parcels.

Kay I felt the call of spring. I went to the sales.

John You seem to have gone berserk. What did you buy?

Kay Three dresses, a divine hat, a housecoat, and some underwear.

John Oh!

Kay All bargains.

John Why do women think they get a bargain at a sale?

Kay appears carrying the tray with tea-things on it. John hurries forward

Kay Here we are.

John Let me take that. (*He takes the tray*) Now what?

Kay (*pointing to the coffee-table*) There!

John Right! (*He takes the tray to the table and puts it down*)

Kay You don't approve of sales?

John I'm a mere man. I think you spend more money buying things you wouldn't buy normally because you are under the impression you're getting a bargain. As soon as you see a ticket marked "reduced from" —you're hooked.

Kay But this was a bargain. (*She goes to the armchair, rummages, and produces a bag*) Now look at this divine hat. (*She pulls it out and puts it on, then goes to the mirror on the wall and surveys the result*) There! (*She does not move from the mirror*)

John Well?

Kay (*turning her head from side to side*) That's funny, in the shop it looked absolutely divine . . .

John And now?

Kay I think it looks perfectly ghastly. What happened to it from Harrods to here?

John Nothing, it's a bargain.

Kay (*putting her hands up to take it off*) It's a . . .

John No, don't take it off.

Kay (*turning*) Why not?

John (*looking at her*) It suits you. It really does.

Kay (*looking at John, then back to the mirror, then back to John again*) We can read Denis Mackail and eat sultana cake together, but I'm damned if I'm wearing this hat. You've slipped, Sir Galahad! (*She takes it off and throws it on a chair, then moves and sits on the couch*) Milk and sugar?

John Please.

Kay (*busy pouring*) Well, sit down and make the place look tidy.

John Thank you. (*He sits beside her*)

Kay (*pouring tea*) Help yourself to sugar.

John Thank you.

Kay (*handing him a cup*) And sultana cake.

John Thank you. (*He takes a piece of cake*) Did you make this?

Kay Yes.

John (*chewing*) It's very nice.

Kay You're living up to your reputation, Sir Galahad. I can't keep on calling you by that ridiculous name. Isn't it about time we introduced ourselves?

John Oh, I'm sorry, you're quite right. It's most remiss of me. (*He puts down his cup*) I'm John Browne.

Kay looks at him quizzically

It really is John Browne. I'll show you my driving licence. It's Browne with an "e".

Kay I'm so relieved about that "e". It makes all the difference. It adds an air of respectability. I'm Kay Brent. (*She holds out her hand*) How do you do?

John (*taking it*) I'm very pleased to meet you.

They solemnly shake hands

Kay Now everything is thoroughly civilized and we have been introduced. We must now talk about the weather.

John It's a beautiful day.

Kay The first day of spring. In the spring a young man's fancy . . . Have some more cake!

John Thank you. (*He takes a piece*) Forgive me asking, but are you—er —er . . .

Kay Married?

John Yes.

Kay No!

John Oh!

Kay Divorced.

John Divorced?

Kay Yes, so no irate husband is going to pop up. You can eat your cake in peace.

John I wasn't worried.

Kay You should have been, or do you often take strange women home? Lurk around sales in your taxi until you see a struggling female loaded with parcels and then gallantly offer the use of your cab?

John (*horrified*) Good heavens, no! I've never done it before. There didn't seem to be any more taxis and you looked so helpless. It was an impulse.

Kay It was lucky for you I only lived a quarter of a mile away. An impulsive act like that could have landed you at Barnet.

John I never thought of that.

Kay With no tea and sultana cake, a jealous husband demanding explanations, and a colossal fare on the taxi meter. You must curb these impulses.

John But I've never done it before.

Kay The first day of spring. There is something in the air today.

John I don't think so. I don't know what made me do it. I really don't.

Kay Don't think about it too much then. You're giving me a large sized inferiority complex already.

John Oh, please—I didn't mean . . . You see, there was I in the taxi—

Kay —and there was I on the pavement.

John —and . . . Well, for that matter, since you didn't know me from Adam why did you get in my taxi?

Kay (*promptly*) My feet ached and I was laden.

John Still, it was a bit risky.

Kay Risky? How?

John Well—well—supposing I'd have—well . . .

Kay What, at three o'clock in the afternoon in the Brompton Road with the driver in front?

John Well . . .

Kay With you in a bowler hat and a pile of parcels between us and passing the Oratory?

John (*embarrassed*) Yes, I suppose it did sound silly. But, I'm very glad you accepted my offer.

Kay Would you be saying that if I lived in Barnet instead of Kensington?

John Even if you lived in Barnet.

Kay (*cheerfully*) Liar!

John That's the truth.

Kay Of course, that goes with the nature badge and tying knots. I'm sorry that sounds very rude and it wasn't meant to be. Of course I believe you. I've got to, I'd be livid otherwise.

John It really is the truth. (*Suddenly*) But it is typical of women to believe what they want to believe . . . (*He looks at Kay and finishes hastily*) If you see what I mean!

Kay (*gurgling with laughter*) And it is typical of men to want them to believe it. Are you married?

John Yes.

Kay (*admiringly*) You really are truthful. Most men would have said no.

John And you would have believed me?

Kay No!

John Why not?

Kay Have some more tea.

John Please.

Kay takes his cup and starts pouring

You haven't answered my question.

Kay You look married.

John How on earth does a man look married?

Kay You have a married look about you.

John A label?

Kay No, just a look. I can't explain it, but a woman can always tell.

John How?

Kay Experience.

John Yours or theirs?

Kay Both! A bachelor is attentive to a woman, but not over-attentive. But a married man with another woman is just that little extra attentive, if you see what I mean.

John No, I don't!

Kay You ask any woman. You ask your wife.

John I couldn't very well ask my wife that. In any case she wouldn't know.

Kay Now that is just typical of married men. They always assume that their wives know nothing about other men.

John My wife . . .

Kay And don't go and really spoil everything by saying you are sure your wife doesn't.

John I wasn't going to.

Kay You were.

John (*after a pause*) Yes, I suppose I was.

Kay (*rising*) I am delighted that you haven't come out with that well known gambit that your wife doesn't understand you.

John Of course not! (*He takes out his cigarette-case and offers it to Kay*) Do you smoke?

Kay I'm afraid so.

Kay takes a cigarette and John gives her a light and then replaces the case and lighter in his pocket

Aren't you?

John I don't! At least, not cigarettes. I sometimes have a cigar, but it has to be a special occasion.

Kay So you keep cigarettes for show—not blow!

John Most of my business friends seem to smoke. Did your husband say that you didn't understand him?

Kay Frequently.

John And did you?

Kay Only too well. I suppose that's why I am divorced. The divorce courts are full of wives who understand misunderstood husbands.

John How long have you been divorced?

Kay Seven years. I was married for fifteen.

John A long time.

Kay Not really. There are such things as silver and diamond weddings. How long have you been married?

John Twenty years.

Kay Happy?

John Yes—yes—I suppose so.

Kay Why, aren't you sure?

John Yes, I am.

Kay Sure or happy?

John Happy! Yes, of course I am.

A slight pause

Kay (*laughing*) Well, don't look so miserable about it.

John I'm not. I was thinking. Were you happy? I mean, happily married?

Kay I thought I was.

John What happened?

Kay He went off with his secretary. He always said she was no damn good as a secretary, but until he went off with her I never realized that she had other qualifications you don't learn at a secretarial college.

John What was he?

Kay A charmer, a real charmer.

John I'm sure he was, but I meant what was he in business.

Kay He's in advertising! Suits him, he's very good at it because he's very persuasive. Have you got a secretary?

John Yes.

Kay What's she like?

John Very efficient.

Kay And that's your secretary.

John Yes, most efficient.

Kay rises and picks up the tray to take back into the kitchen

(*Rising*) Please let me take that.

Kay Thank you, but don't go all domesticated and start washing up.

John takes the tray and moves into the kitchen.

(*Mischievously*) Have you ever been to bed with her?

John, still holding tray, comes back into the room

John (*horrified*) I beg your pardon?

Kay I said, have you ever been to bed with her?

John Good heavens no! (*He goes back into the kitchen, deposits the tray and comes back into the room*)

Kay Have you ever wanted to?

John Certainly not! Never!

Kay That proves it!

John Proves what!

Kay If you have never even thought about it she must be mousy, a spinster, and over fifty. Right?

John Well—yes! But she is very efficient.

Kay Poor woman! Have you ever taken her out to dinner?

John No! Her entire private life is completely centred around her church. Bible classes, Mothers' Union ...

Kay Mothers' Union? But she's a spinster, how did she get in?

John I believe the term mother is used rather loosely in this connection.

Kay It all sounds very suspicious to me.

John Actually, she is secretary to the Mothers' Union.

Kay It appears to be a very odd set up. Do the Mothers show no discrimination? I bet she adores you.

John Miss Adams? My God! I hope not.

Kay She does. And she puts flowers on your desk.

John How did you know?

Kay I guessed.

John She's been with me for fifteen years and I haven't the heart to tell her that I can't stand flowers on my desk.

Kay Never tell her. That's proof of her adoration. You are probably the one romantic spot in her life.

John I hate to disillusion you, but I think the Vicar holds that position.

Kay What's she like?

John Rather like you described her, only more so.

Kay No, I meant your wife.

John I thought we were talking about my secretary, Miss Adams.

Kay No, I just wondered what your wife was like. That's rather rude of me, isn't it, on such a short acquaintance.

John The whole acquaintance has been mad anyway, and I can't say you have been exactly reticent in your questions.

Kay (*giggling*) I'm sorry, I must sound terribly rude.

John No, no! Just—just—well—unusual.

Kay Well, what's she like?

John My wife? (*Pause*) She's nice. Yes, she's very nice.

Kay Please, please, you embarrass me by your unbridled passion.

John Well, dammit, what can a man say? She's—well—as I said—very nice.

Kay (*casually*) What are the colour of her eyes?

John opens his mouth to speak, then closes it, thinks, then eventually speaks

John Brown.

Kay You are absolutely sure?

John Yes, yes, of course I am.

Kay They're brown.

John (*hesitantly*) Ye—e—s. (*Then determinedly*) Yes!

Kay (*turning away*) What colour are mine?

John (*promptly*) Blue.

Kay Sure?

John Of course I am. I've just been looking at them. They're blue.

Kay (*turning back again*) You're right! And your wife's eyes are hazel.

John Yes, hazel, that's right.

Kay But you said, just now, that they were brown.

John sits slowly and carefully on the arm of the couch

John (*speaking slowly and distinctly*) I see you struggling with parcels and I have the last taxi. For some inexplicable reason I offer to take you home, and for some equally inexplicable reason you accept. We arrive at your flat and you ask me to stay to tea. We indulge in a certain amount of light-hearted small-talk. Then out of the blue you suddenly ask me the colour of my wife's eyes and I'm right, slap-bang, in the middle of a third degree. (*Slapping his hand violently on his knee*) And I don't like it! And do you know why?

Fascinated, Kay shakes her head

I'm damned if I can remember the exact colour of her eyes. I've been looking at them for over twenty years. They're eyes! I've accepted them, they're normal eyes. I haven't thought about their colour. Now you've got me worried.

Kay I bet your wife knows the colour of yours.

John That's right, make it worse! She's got brown hair.

Kay Hooray!

John I mean, brown hair means brown eyes, doesn't it?

Kay Or hazel.

John Well, they're not blue. I'm sure of that.

Kay Are you?

John (*helplessly*) I don't think I'm sure of anything any more.

Kay Except that she's got brown hair.

John (*with conviction*) Yes, brown hair.

Kay I hate to throw you into more confusion, but what's her name? If you're not quite sure or it escapes you at the moment, don't worry. I shall quite understand.

John It's Enid.

Kay That sounds definite enough. Enid!

John Yes, Enid Mary.

Kay I'm really getting to know your wife. Her name is Enid Mary Browne, with an "e". She has brown, without an "e", hair. Her eyes are brown, perhaps hazel, but definitely not blue.

John You're laughing at me.

Kay (*giggling*) Yes, I am, in a nice sort of way. You are so typical.

John Of what?

Kay Of men, comfortably married men. You are all good, kind, solid, dependable. (*Suddenly*) When is Enid's birthday?

John (*promptly*) March the ninth.

Kay That is really marvellous! You are forgiven, really forgiven, for all your other failures. A man who remembers his wife's birthday is really exceptional. My ex-husband never remembered mine.

John Thank you.

Kay Not at all. Credit where credit is due. When is your wedding anniversary?

John (*hesitantly*) August the tenth, or the twentieth, I can never remember which. But it doesn't matter, she always reminds me.

Kay John Browne, with an "e", you've slipped again. How is it you remember her birthday?

John (*sheepishly*) Well, by a strange coincidence, it's the same day as mine.

Kay You fraud!

John Oh come, be fair! Admit that I could have said I wasn't married. Having said I was, I could have said any colour for my wife's eyes. In fact, I could have said anything about anything, couldn't I?

Kay True! I stand corrected.

John Good! (*Rising*) I'd better go.

Kay Why? I'm sorry, have I offended you?

John (*sitting down again*) No, I just thought I had stayed long enough.

Kay Well, if you want to go, or have an appointment . . . Where were you off to in a taxi, anyway?

John An appointment.

Kay Have you missed it?

John Yes, I was late then. That's why I took a taxi.

Kay And you missed an appointment to help me?

John Yes. (*Gallantly*) But it was worth it.

Kay (*contritely*) I feel terrible, I really do. When I think of some of the things I've said. (*She suddenly sits on the couch*) I feel that big! (*She puts her finger and thumb very slightly apart*) I've put you on the witness stand, I've said . . . Oh, what have I said! But that's me. I just ask questions—bang, bang—please or offend. Just because I like people and want to know them. I'm so very sorry! Was it important that appointment?

John It was, rather.

Kay (*horrified*) Don't, don't! You make me feel worse. You're a business man, aren't you?

John Yes, I am.

Kay Oh my God! I've probably lost you a big contract. I've cost you thousands of pounds.

John What did an appointment matter when I was able to assist you.

Kay Thank you. (*She suddenly rises and moves forward and kisses John's cheek*) There! (*She steps back*)

John looks astonished

That's a bit of jam on the sultana cake to show how sorry I am. Who was the appointment with?

John My dentist. I was glad of the excuse.

Kay (*furiously*) John Browne, I take back everything I said and did. I was just the excuse you were looking for to miss an appointment with your dentist. That's bad enough, but that's not the worst. Oh, no! (*Pointing an accusing finger*) You are a coward! A typical man, frightened of a bit of pain. A coward.

John (*reflectively*) Y'know, I've come to the conclusion that your ex-husband's secretary must have been a very sweet girl.

Kay Eh?

John Appealing, feminine, and helpless, which gave him the urge to protect her. Probably quiet, too.

Kay looks at him then suddenly laughs

Touché!

John (*laughing too*) Was she?

Kay All that and a blonde to boot!

John Obviously.

Kay But she's a cow now, if you'll forgive the expression. Extravagant and a born nagger. I had lunch with him the other day and he poured out all his troubles to me.

John And how were you?

Kay Sweet, feminine and sympathetic.

John In actual fact, you were being a bit of a cow, too.

Kay Not really, I did feel sympathetic. He didn't deserve it, but then he didn't deserve Helen either. I could afford sympathy. I also felt excessively noble.

John Would you take him back?

Kay (*cheerfully*) No!

John Why not?

Kay Because I'm very happy as I am. I've had the *hors d'oeuvres* and the main course, I'm on the sweets now.

John If that means what I think it means, you have a delicate way of expressing yourself.

Kay I thought it was rather nice, too.

The telephone rings

John A *crêpes suzette*?

Kay Eh? (*She laughs*) No, probably the main course. He said he was going to ring me. Excuse me. (*She picks up the receiver*) Hallo, Kensington eight-one-seven-two. . . . Darling, how are you? How nice of you to ring. . . . Have you? I was out shopping. . . . When? Yes, I'd love to. . . . That's a date then. Dinner on Friday. Pick me up here and have a drink before we leave. . . . Sevenish? . . . Lovely. Look forward to seeing you. . . . 'Bye, darling! (*She replaces the receiver*) A date!

John A date?

Kay A date!

John It was a *crêpes suzette*, then.

Kay No, bicarbonate of soda. That was Mavis, my dearest friend.

John Why the bicarb?

Kay She thinks sweets are bad for me.

John She's the still small voice of conscience?

Kay Not Mavis! She might think they're bad for me, but she takes a hell of an interest in them.

John (*a little stiffly*) You sound as though you are going through the menu.

Kay (*stepping on to the couch and sitting on the arm*) You are getting the wrong impression. You have already come to the conclusion that I am a cross between a nymphomaniac and a female Dracula.

John I assure you I haven't.

Kay (*cheerfully wagging her finger at him*) John Browne, you're a liar! You have! You will go home to your wife and say! "I met a scarlet woman today, a positive sex maniac!"

John Can you imagine me saying that to my wife over the dinner table?

Kay No, and consequently you won't.

John Why not? I could certainly tell her about this little adventure.

Kay (*looking at him with her head on one side*) Oh, you never would. Now be honest! Remember the badge you won as a Boy Scout (*She gives the Scout sign*)—clean in thought, word, and deed.

John (*indignantly*) I strongly resent the inference that my behaviour has been such that I would hesitate to tell my wife.

Kay Hooray! Bully for you! Then you are going to tell her.

John (*after a pause, briefly*) No!

Kay goes off into peals of laughter and John looks uncomfortable

I don't see anything to laugh at.

Kay (*wiping her eyes*) I'm sorry, I really am, but . . . (*Suddenly she goes off into peals of laughter again*)

John (*dignified*) I fail to see anything amusing in anything I've said.

Kay (*recovering*) I'm sorry! Oh Lor', I seem to be apologizing every other sentence. But you vacillate.

John I can be accused of many things, but I do not vacillate.

Kay But you've just vacillated! That doesn't sound grammatical, anyway, you've changed your mind.

John That is not vacillating!

Kay Then what is it?

John (*taking a deep breath*) It's . . .

Kay I mean in plain English, not addressing a board meeting or dictating a letter to Miss Adams.

John (*patiently*) It means that everything that has happened since we met, however illogical, seems logical here and now with you. But to go home and tell my wife all that has happened, however logical, will become illogical when I explain it to her. So . . . (*He gestures with the air of a man who has made everything crystal clear*)

Kay (*gazing at him fascinatedly*) And that's plain English?

John I thought so.

Kay I gather that you are not telling Enid about me.

John I have just explained . . .

Kay If you explain to her about me as you've explained to me why you aren't telling her, you've got nothing to worry about.

John Why not?

Kay She'll be as baffled as I am and just say "Yes, dear!" But it's entirely up to you. Is she the jealous sort? Y'know, the type that says sweetly —"It would never worry me if John looked at another woman"—with the underlying inference "God help him if he does!" Or is she tactful, takes things as they come, and like Nelson, puts the telescope to her blind eye?

John I don't know.

Kay (*amazed*) You don't know! After twenty years.

John No! (*As one working out a problem*) I set out from my office to go to my dentist . . .

Kay You haven't a toothache, have you?

John No, just a check-up.

Kay I'm so glad.

John And what happens to me? On an impulse I give a strange woman—

Kay An attractive lady—

John —an attractive lady . . .

Kay That sounds much better. That gives the reason for the impulse.

John It doesn't give the reason for anything.

Kay So if I'd have been fat, sixty, and ugly as well, I could have still counted on a lift?

John (*doubtfully*) Well . . .

Kay Scouts' honour!

John Oh dammit . . .

Kay Good, that's settled. Resume your most interesting narrative, my dear Watson. On an impulse you gave an attractive lady—

John —a lift . . .

There is a long pause

Kay Well, now where are we? Am I still outside Harrods, in the cab, or have we arrived back here yet?

John We're here.

Kay Good! This is where it gets interesting.

John This is where it goes crazy. We start off with casual small talk—

Kay *Greenery Street*, sultana cake—

John —and before I know were I am I'm suddenly asked, among other things, if I've been to bed with my secretary. Nobody's ever asked me that before.

Kay They've probably seen Miss Adams, I haven't, and I was curious.

John But it is not the usual question one is asked by a perfect stranger after half an hour's conversation.

Kay And you have answered my questions.

John That is what I don't understand.

Kay And you've asked a few yourself.

John And I don't understand that either.

Kay And I answered them. We've had a most friendly conversation.

John Oh, is that what it was?

Kay Yes, and for some extraordinary reason you aren't telling your wife.

John No!

Kay Why not! Attractive women don't bother her, and I might be looked upon as a pretty girl to whom you have been most pleasant.

John This is different. She might not understand.

Kay Ah-ha!

John If I don't understand why I gave you a lift in the first place, why should she?

Kay It's the first day of spring and that does things to people. Perhaps there's a magic in the air. Never mind, you'll be back to normal tomorrow.

John (*indignantly*) I'm normal now. I've just slipped out of my groove, that's all.

Kay (*starting to laugh*) Now don't start me laughing again . . .

John Now what's funny?

Kay You slipping out of the groove of your well ordered existence, however briefly, John Browne, with the respectable little "e". What is your existence?

John (*in despair*) Here we go again!

Kay Never mind, it's the first day of spring. Back to normal tomorrow, but it's still today, so . . . You are a businessman.

John Yes.

Kay What?

John I am a director of a publishing firm.

Kay Office hours nine till five.

John I said I was a director, ten till five.

Kay Where do you live?

John Hampstead.

Kay The picture is getting clearer. Belong to a golf club as well, I expect!

John Yes, handicap ten.

Kay Not bad! Go out much?

John Occasional dinners, business and social. Oh, and we visit friends for bridge. I play a lot of bridge!

Kay I thought you might. Clubs?

John Army and Navy, not night.

Kay Children?

John One son, Simon, at college.

Kay A well-ordered existence. Any affairs. *Crêpes suzettes*, or should I say, peach melbas?

John (*horrified*) Good heavens, no!

Kay What never?

John No, never!

Kay Not even a teeny-weeny one?

John It is perhaps conceivable that I am content with the main course. (*He stops*) Oh my God! That doesn't sound like me at all. (*Accusingly*) But then, I'm quoting you.

Kay I know, I'm the terrible one.

John Not really. I suppose you are just unique.

Kay I wouldn't say so.

John Perhaps you seem so to me because of my well ordered existence. I haven't met anyone quite like you before.

Kay People like me don't usually make up a four at bridge. Anyhow, in spite of my peculiarities it's been perhaps worthwhile after all.

John (*a shade wistfully*) Yes. (*He rises with an air of reluctance*) Well, I suppose I'd better go, it's nearly four o'clock. I have some letters to dictate and Miss Adams will be waiting. As you said, back to normal tomorrow.

Kay Yes! Any attractive ladies outside Harrods tomorrow struggling with parcels can go to blazes.

John I won't even notice them. (*He goes to the window-seat, picks up his overcoat and puts it on*) Could I lend you my copy of *The Young Livingstones*?

Kay I'd love to read it again. How do I return it? I mean, you can't have that popping up on the breakfast table at Hampstead without questions being asked. I'm bound to put in a note of thanks and I have a very feminine hand.

John (*diffidently*) Perhaps I could call and collect it sometime?

Kay Do you really think you'll want to? You'll be well and truly back in your groove then with only vague memories of the scarlet woman.

John I do not consider you a scarlet woman.

Kay Pale pink then. Yes, do please call and collect it.

John Good, I'll send it to you.

John moves to the door and with hand on latch, turns to Kay, who has followed him

Until our next meeting then. I mean, to collect the book.

Kay I gathered that.

John Well, good-bye, Mrs Brent. (*He opens the door*)

Kay Good-bye, John.

John Oh, I should say *au revoir*—Kay.

Kay *Au revoir*, John.

John exits

Oh, John!

John (*off*) Yes?

Kay I should tell you that I am a very quick reader.

Kay gently closes the door as—

the CURTAIN *falls*

Scene 2

The same. A June afternoon

The only radical alteration in the room is that the vase on the telephone table is filled with summer flowers

When the Curtain *rises the stage is empty, but it is bright with summer sunshine. After a moment there is laughter off stage, then the front door opens and John is seen taking the key out of the lock. Kay passes him and enters. She is dressed in a gay summer dress and she is wearing the hat she thought "ghastly" in Scene 1. John is still soberly dressed, but in a light-weight summer suit and he carries the inevitable bowler hat*

Kay (*laughing, as she rushes in, collapses on the couch and takes off her hat*) I tell you it was the same driver that brought us here the first time.

John (*closing the door, coming down to the telephone table and dropping the keys on it*) You couldn't possibly recognize him after three months.

Kay I recognized the back of his head.

John (*moving up to the window-seat and dropping his bowler hat on it*) I would hardly call the back of his head distinctive.

Kay It was! It was all criss-crossed with little lines like Clapham Junction. I thought the first time that I saw him, "Poor man, if that's the back of your head, what's your face like?"

John (*sitting on the couch*) And what was it like?

Kay Oliver Cromwell's.

John Oliver Cromwell's?

Kay Yes, he had two warts. A most distinctive taxi-driver, and I recognized him at once. I mean, two warts do take a bit of forgetting. I think he recognized us, too.

John Naturally, as soon as he saw us he said to himself, "Ah" I picked up this couple three months ago—"

Kay "—I distinctly remember that very attractive lady—"

John "—and—and . . ." (*He stops*)

Kay Don't be silly, Oliver must have thought something about you, too.

John I doubt whether Oliver, or any man for that matter, would notice me when you're around.

Kay Ooooooh! That sounds like the beginning of a lovely compliment. Go on, don't stop now.

John Well—well . . . (*He flounders*)

Kay Go on, force yourself, darling. Throw caution to the winds. I love flattery, I fall for it every time.

John Flattery means to praise falsely, or unduly; to raise false hopes.

Kay Not to a woman, except of course, if it comes from another woman. From a man it always sounds like the truth.

John That depends on the man.

Kay Don't you believe it, my dear. That's the one time a man's voice carries the ring of conviction.

John Oh?
Kay Because he's trying to convince the woman.
John Is he?
Kay Yes! Usually for one basic reason, and you can't get more basic than *that*.
John (*stiffly*) That's really going a bit too far!
Kay (*laughing*) You've gone all dignified. (*She suddenly swings her legs beneath her and kneels on the couch looking at him*) I've shocked you.
John Well, I do think you shouldn't generalize and jump to conclusions.
Kay I love shocking you because you fall for it every time. (*Coaxingly*) I'm sorry! Now, you started off by paying me a compliment. How would you define a compliment?
John (*slightly mollified*) Well, a compliment is an act of courtesy. It shows respect and regard.
Kay Ah, that sounds much better. I'm all for that. (*She sits back on her heels*) I really believe compliments.

A pause

Well, come on! I'm waiting to be complimented.
John Well—well—what I meant was . . .
Kay One of your most endearing qualities is your gay spontaneity.
John Dammit, how can I be spontaneous now? That means involuntary. I just thought of something before and said it involuntarily.
Kay Lovely! Now think of something else quickly and say that.
John How the devil can I with you kneeling there with practically a stop watch in your hand. It's a wonder you haven't started a count-down.
Kay Would a drink help?
John (*with relief*) I don't say it would be a help, but it would be very welcome.
Kay Then you shall have one. Whisky and soda?
John Please.
Kay (*moving across to the drinks cabinet*) I'm running a bit short of whisky, but I can just about manage it. I'm expecting supplies to be delivered this afternoon.

Kay gets out glasses and starts pouring drinks. John watches her

That was a lovely lunch, thank you. You really do know the nicest places to eat, all cosy and intimate, even at lunch times. I think Padonni's is my favourite after all. If I didn't know you better I'd swear you had secret lunch time sessions before.
John (*suddenly, speaking quietly as he looks at her*) You are so beautiful, so very beautiful.

Kay slowly turns and looks at him

Kay (*also quietly*) Now that was nice. I believe that.
John You think you are beautiful?
Kay No! Oh, I'm attractive, I know that. But I believe I am beautiful to you and I'm glad.

John That wasn't—flattery.

Kay I know, you really meant it, my dear. (*She moves to the couch, carrying the glasses. On reaching it she kneels on it again beside John and hands him a glass*) Do you realize that this is the first time you have unbent and become intimate.

John (*startled*) Intimate?

Kay How many times have I seen you?

John A few, I suppose. Yes, a few.

Kay (*raising her eyes to heaven in mute appeal*) A few he says. To be precise, since we first met, I've had twenty luncheons with you in ten weeks.

John Have you?

Kay Today was the twenty-first.

John Was it? I haven't kept count. I like taking you out to lunch.

Kay I like to go. I like eating and I like eating with you. But today was the twenty-first. Rather like a coming of age. The opening up of a new world.

John I just thought it was a very pleasant lunch.

Kay But it must have been an occasion to you.

John Why?

Kay You smoked a cigar, and you said you only smoke those on special occasions.

John Haven't I smoked one before?

Kay Not with me you haven't.

John Oh!

Kay So I thought today was special.

John Well, it was!

Kay I knew it!

John Yes, I managed to get the full publishing rights of a fabulous new novel and we signed the contract today. I meant to tell you about it.

Kay Oh, and I thought you were beginning to unbend.

John Because I smoked a cigar?

Kay No, because just now you unbent.

John Did I?

Kay You said I was beautiful.

John (*defiantly*) Well, that's what I think. (*He hastily gulps down his drink*)

Kay You'll get hiccups, and I don't want you hiccupping when you are about to kiss me.

John hastily rises

Now where are you off to—?

John (*moving in the direction of the bathroom door*) I was just going to . . .

Kay This is a fine time to be going to the loo!

John (*shouting*) I am not going to the loo.

Kay (*shouting*) Then where are you going?

John I was going to get myself another drink.

Kay (*jumping off the couch*) That's the way to the loo. The drinks are in the opposite direction.

John I was working my way around gradually.

Kay Oh my God!

Kay suddenly sits down in the corner of the couch and rests her arm on the arm and props her face in her hand. John moves over to the drinks cabinet and picks up the whisky bottle

John There's no more whisky.

Kay (*not looking at him and without moving her position*) I said I was running out.

John Oh! Ah well! (*He stands fiddling with his glass*)

Kay (*in the same position, just raising her left arm with the glass*) Take mine, I haven't touched it.

John I couldn't take yours.

Kay Why not?

John Well—you may want it.

Kay I probably will.

John Well, there you are then.

Kay Yes, here I am, but where are you?

John Over here. I'm looking for a drink.

Kay (*still in the same position*) There's brandy, sherry, gin and orangeade, all to hand. There is even a bottle of "Passion Fruit", but for God's sake don't touch that it might go to your head. However, if you fancy a cup of tea and you want to do your usual working-around-gradually act, you can get to the kitchenette via my bedroom, through the door in there into the loo, then through the loo out of that door, and you'll see the kitchenette straight ahead.

John There is no need for sarcasm, I'll have a brandy.

Kay You do that.

John very slowly gets out the brandy. He gets another glass. Carefully he pours a measure, carefully replaces the bottle and closes the cabinet door. He then stands holding the glass cupped in his hands. There is quite a silence. Eventually Kay speaks

He can't have left because I would have heard the front door close. He's probably passed out, the brandy was too much for him.

John You know damn well I'm over here.

Kay (*in a sudden burst of exasperation*) Oh! (*She slams her glass down on the table, leaps to her feet and faces John*) Oh, you—you—I have known you for ten weeks. In ten weeks we have had twenty-one luncheons. With twenty-one luncheons I have gone through the menu from Escargots to Shrimp Cocktail, from Châteaubriand to Lobster Cardinal, and from Strawberry Romanoff to Crème Caramel. I have drunk Don Perignon to Mouton Rothschild, and Château Y'quem down to beer even. The only thing that hasn't varied, apart from you, has been the coffee and that's because I always have it black. I have heard of your working day in detail, and I know what old Bassett, the Managing Director, said to you and what you said to old Bassett. Miss Adams has almost become an intimate friend, and her Vicar can practically expect a Christmas card from me. I have never seen your garden but I know where your roses are, the petunias, and every other flower, and I know the trouble you have with your lawn. I know the man next door to you on your left is a retired admiral, a bore with the mentality of a half-wit, because two weeks ago he trumped your ace. I know that the man on the other side is a jolly good type and that you play golf with him. If all the members of your golf club were to come through that door now I could identify every damn one of them. And do you know what? I couldn't bloody well care less! (*Her voice during this speech has risen and she picks up a cushion from the window-seat and goes to hurl it at John*)

John (*who has been gazing at her fascinatedly, half ducks*) Here, I say, I'm sorry . . .

Kay (*suddenly she gives a little laugh and tosses the cushion back on the window-seat*) Oh my dear, you really are . . . (*She goes to him and takes his glass and puts it on top of the cabinet*) You won't need that! (*She puts her arm through his and leads him back to the couch*)

John I don't quite understand . . .

Kay (*seating herself beside him on the couch*) No, darling, I'm the one that doesn't understand. I really don't.

John But you see . . .

John is very conscious of Kay's proximity, he sits gazing ahead with his hands on his knees. Kay turns sideways and looks at him

Kay After every luncheon we come back here and sit on this couch together as we are now. Well, almost! And what do you do?

John Nothing!

Kay (*putting her arm slowly around his shoulders*) Exactly! You talk some more about any little thing that might have escaped your memory over lunch, and at four o'clock you depart.

John Miss Adams is waiting for . . .

Kay (*very gently stroking the back of his head*) For twenty meetings this has happened with unfailing regularity. (*Gently rubbing her cheek against his*) I sometimes wonder whether I should suddenly take off my clothes to arouse some interest in you.

John I say, really . . .

Kay (*murmuring into his ear*) But it wouldn't be worth it, and you wouldn't notice anyway.

John Oh, but I . . .

Kay (*from here on making full play for him*) But today you suddenly forgot yourself. Today you unbent. Today you went positively berserk and you said I was beautiful. I grabbed that fleeting moment. And then what happened?

John You—you—said I was about to—to—kiss you.

Kay Then what did you do? You got up hastily and wandered around looking for a drink like Moses looking for the promised land. And he was about as unlucky as I was. (*She now has her arm around John, leaning against him and forcing him down on the couch*)

John is right down on the couch with his head resting on the arm. Kay is almost lying across him. One arm around him, the other hand gently stroking his face. Her mouth is very close to his

Some men consider even one luncheon and a seat on my couch practically an invitation into my bed, and one has to tactfully, or otherwise, dispel their illusions.

John's arm begins to slowly go around Kay

But if a man asks me out as often as you have done, and I go, I take it he has more interest in me than seeing how I hold my knife and fork.

John (*weakly*) You hardly ever use a knife. You have that shocking American habit of only using a fork.

Kay jerks away and freezes, then suddenly flings her arms in the air in despair

Kay (*her voice building*) I don't believe it, I just don't believe it. I have hinted, I have cajoled, I have implored this man, and all he says is—I have a nasty habit with my fork. (*She rises and moves abruptly away from him*)

John is left lying on the couch

John Browne, will you promise to answer me one question honestly? A plain forthright yes or no!

John (*nervously, slowly sitting up*) It depends what it is.

Kay Do you promise?

John Well—yes!

Kay Do you want to make love to me? Yes or no!

John Well . . .

Kay (*stamping her feet*) Yes or no!

John (*shouting*) You know damn well I do!

Kay Then come and do something about it.

John quickly rises and moves to her, and they are in each other's arms. They kiss passionately

(*Breathlessly*) It can now be officially stated that John Browne has unbent. (*She kisses him gently*) I almost thought . . .

She cannot finish her sentence as John is once more kissing her passionately

Darling, darling, I know that you are making up for lost time, but this is ridiculous.

John Why is it?

Kay It's only two-thirty now and you don't have to dash off to dictate your letters to Miss Adams until four o'clock.

John Damn the letters and damn Miss Adams.

They kiss passionately again

Kay If she could see you now, that would be something to tell the Vicar.

John goes to kiss her again but Kay holds him off

My love, with a bed in walking distance and a couch in easy reach, do we have to stand in the middle of the room? I do like my creature comforts, particularly at moments like this. Which is it to be?

John Oh, you mean couch—or—or . . .

Kay Bed! It's quite a popular piece of house furnishing. No home should be without one.

John I think . . .

Kay Bed?

John (*hastily*) No, couch! Couch!

Kay I don't know why I even bothered to mention the other. (*She pulls John towards the couch*) Well, come on! Half a loaf . . .

Once on the couch there is another passionate kiss and they both sink on it

Now why haven't you done this before? Didn't you want to?

John Of course I did.

Kay You took long enough to make up your mind. Do you take twenty-one board meetings before you reach a decision, darling?

John This isn't business, darling!

Kay True, but you could call it a merger, my sweet!

Kay kisses John again

John (*breaking slightly away*) There are one or two things to be considered . . . (*He rises and moves away*)

Kay Oh my God, he's off on his travels again. Or are you going to my bedroom?

John Of course not.

Kay Otherwise I'd follow you. Are you sure?

John Of course I am. I'm not!

Kay Then for heaven's sake forget the gypsy in you and come and sit down.

John I—I—want to talk . . .

Kay Now he wants to talk! (*Jumping up*) You choose the most extra-ordinary moments for a discussion. Right in the middle of our first love making you want to talk.

John I want to get certain things clear.

Kay And a fine time you've chosen. Well, I suppose going to bed with you will improve my intellect.

John Is it not conceivable that we should discuss matters before taking such a big decision?

Kay (*shouting*) I bet you are the only man in the world who would use a bed as a debating platform.

John (*shouting*) We are not in bed.

Kay You're telling me!

John I suppose we can talk sometimes.

Kay We've had twenty sometimes. All right, all right, let's talk. (*She sits determinedly in an armchair, bolt upright and folds her arms*) Well now, how do you feel about the Common Market?

John (*shouting*) I want to talk about us. Us!

Kay (*gravely nodding her head*) By all means. I am sure we have many points of mutual interest, although I must admit I cannot think of one at the moment. However, have you read any good books lately? The other day I read—

John (*shouting*) I don't want to be a *crêpes suzette*.

Kay —a book about —— (*She breaks off*) Be a what?

John (*suddenly embarrassed*) You know, a *crêpes suzette*.

Kay I know what a *crêpes suzette* is, it's an expensive type of pancake.

John You know what I mean, and I don't want to be one.

Kay (*humouring a child*) And you shan't be a *crêpes suzette*, or a rice pudding . . .

John (*striding across to her*) You are being deliberately obtuse. You know damn well what I mean.

Kay (*jumping up*) I do not know what you mean.

John Well, you should. I hate to feel I am becoming one of your sweets after the main course—and that's your elegant phrasing, not mine.

John turns and flings himself down on the couch

Kay (*comprehending*) Oh that!

John Yes, that!

Kay Is that why it's taken you so long to get around to kissing me?

John Partly that—yes.

Kay looks at him, then gives a quiet little laugh, moves across and kneels again on the couch

Kay Darling, darling John! (*Her hand gently strokes his face*) I've suddenly dropped into the quiet pool of your existence and created a maelstrom. (*She leans forward and kisses his cheek*) Now! (*Back to her old gaiety, she swings around and sits on the arm at the far end of the couch*) John Browne, with the funny little "e", you've got the wrong opinion of me. Deep down in your heart you think I'm a cross between Messalina, Cleopatra and Fanny Hill!

John I never said you were.

Kay You don't have to say it. And I tell you also, quite frankly. I am not Miss Adams either.

John I found that out very early on.

Kay But my life is not one succession of hectic affairs.

John But you've had them.

Kay Of course I have. If you must know, I've had four in seven years. The last one was two years ago. Nobody would ever say to me, "Get thee to a nunnery", and persuade me to go. I like sex. I approve of it. It's one of life's enjoyments that the Government hasn't got around to taxing yet—at least, not directly—and I need it.

John I'm certainly not narrow-minded, but sometimes you . . .

Kay (*standing up on the couch suddenly, looking down on him and shouting*) Darling! So help me, I'll throw something at you in a moment. I like

the theatre, I approve of it, and I need it; but I don't go to the Old Vic
every night.

John I fail to see any comparison between sex and the Old Vic. That's
practically a national institution.

Kay (*giggling*) So?

John What I mean is ... Oh, dammit, darling, it's all right for you.
You're used to this, I'm not. (*He rises and wanders around the room*)
Why the hell did you have to run out of whisky?

Kay (*pointing to her glass on the table*) Take mine. You need it more than
I do.

John (*picking up her glass*) Thanks! (*He drinks*) You see, there are some
men, married men I mean, who—who—well, believe it or not—have—
well, never had an affair. I'm one of them. (*Defiantly*) You can laugh!

Kay I wasn't going to.

John (*wandering again with his whisky*) Because of that, I—I—feel, well,
not so much embarrassed—as, well, frightened of making a fool of
myself. One knows about affairs, one hears about them from—from . . .

Kay The golf club?

John Partly—yes.

Kay I bet they're a real lot of devils!

John Anyhow, now it's happened to me. To me!!

Kay We haven't had an affair. Half a dozen kisses don't constitute an affair.

John (*still wandering*) No, but—well, it's obvious that something's going
to happen.

Kay It might be to you.

John Isn't it to you?

Kay Not at the moment.

John Well, what do you think I'm doing?

Kay God only knows!

John Now look, darling . . .

Kay I'm confused. You work at such speed you don't give a girl a chance
to think. In a matter of a mere short ten weeks you suddenly kiss me for
a minute and a half. I'm not used to such quick action. It might only
be another ten or eleven weeks before you kiss me again. (*Her voice
rises*) And a matter of a mere five years before we actually start the
affair. In the meantime, will you please stop orbiting around my flat
like a lost sputnik. You're driving me mad! And give me that glass, I
need that drop of whisky.

John Oh, yes!

John hands Kay the glass and she drains it

Kay Thank you!

*Kay hands the glass back to John and he stands looking at her. Kay reseats
herself on the arm of the couch and surveys him*

At least, for a moment, you are static, thank God!

John I'm sorry, darling, it's a habit of mine to move when I'm thinking.
I move around when I'm dictating.

Kay Would you like us to take a stroll around the flat together? I'll get my walking shoes on, these pinch a bit.

John (*mentally wrestling, starting to move again*) You see, my world's turned upside down. It's not that I don't want you, I do.

Kay Good! (*She rises and solemnly walks along behind him*)

John I've often thought of what might happen between us, I mean, I never thought it would—but I just thought. And now it's happened—well, when I say happened. I mean—well, I should say . . .

Kay Damn all's happened.

John (*swinging around and seeing her*) What are you doing?

Kay If you're going to spend the entire afternoon walking I might as well keep you company. We'll be passing the kitchenette soon, we might pop in for a cup of tea.

John (*taking her in his arms*) I don't want a cup of tea.

They kiss

Kay Hooray! You've unbent again.

John kisses her again

I don't think you do want tea.

John Not at the moment.

Kay Good! One has to grab the fleeting moment before it passes with you. Darling, darling John, I love you, I love you. I really do. (*She lightly kisses him*) God knows why, but I do.

John I love you too, Kay, my darling.

Kay You really are unbending.

John (*releasing her and moving away*) This has never happened to me before and . . .

Kay (*moving forward and grabbing him*) Oh no you don't. We've had all that and you're wearing out my carpet.

John (*putting his arms around her again*) The trouble is, I haven't got a conscience and I feel I should have. It worries me. I feel I should be worried.

Kay And are you?

John No! That's what worries me.

Kay Darling, if you want to sit down and worry as to why you're not worried, please do. I am going into my bedroom . . .

Kay kisses him passionately, then turns and goes straight into her bedroom and closes the door

John suddenly sits on the couch. After a moment he turns and looks at the bedroom door. He takes out his handkerchief and wipes his forehead. Suddenly rises with a grim air of determination and moves towards the bedroom, then abruptly changes course and hurries to the drink cabinet. He hastily gets out the brandy and a glass and pours himself a generous measure and gulps it down. Again he looks at the bedroom and slowly removes his jacket and tie and drops them on the couch. He slowly moves towards the bedroom door and suddenly there is a ring at the front door

*For a moment John stands petrified, and then he turns and goes to the
kitchenette, closes the door and stands leaning against it. The bedroom
door opens and Kay comes out in a négligé.*

Kay (*looking around, surprised*) Where . . . ? (*She moves over to the
kitchenette door*) Relax darling, it's the boy with the drinks.

*Kay goes to the front door and opens it wide as John slowly opens the
kitchenette door. The open front door reveals Mavis who swoops in, and
John, panic-stricken, hastily closes the door again. Mavis is a very plump,
fashionably dressed woman, in her late forties. She is heavily made-up
and is obviously making a gallant attempt to fight increasing age, but
not very successfully*

Mavis (*swooping in*) Darling! I'm so glad to find you in. There was I in
the Brompton Road simply dying for a cup of tea, and I suddenly
thought, "Kay's bound to be in, I'll call on her for a chatty chat". So I
did, and here I am. Kay, darling, how are you?

Kay I . . .

*Kay closes the front door and makes a gesture as though she is about to
strangle Mavis and hastily drops her hands as Mavis turns*

Mavis You're looking quite, quite ravishing, and that négligé suits you.
What a pity there is only little me to see it.

Kay Yes, I . . .

Mavis (*carrying on*) Every time I see you I think "How does she keep her
figure?" God! This hot weather plays merry hell with my feet. (*She sinks
into an armchair and proceeds to kick off her shoes*) Oooooh the relief!
Either my feet swell or these shoes are too damn tight. You always look
so cool and immaculate. How the hell do you do it? All I do is swell
and perspire. Kay, my love, how are you? You haven't told me.

Kay I haven't had a chance, but I'm . . .

Mavis You're right, I do talk. God! My feet! I've been tramping Kensington looking for a present for George.

*Mavis bends over and proceeds to massage her feet. At the same time Kay
sees John's coat and tie on the couch and whips them up and holds them
behind her*

It's his birthday tomorrow. He's fifty, my dear, fifty. Can you believe
it! He's reached his half century and nearly his allotted span, poor devil.

*During the above speech Kay moves to the kitchenette door behind Mavis's
back, opens it quickly and thrusts in John's coat and tie. John hastily begins
to don them*

Kay Did you get George's present?

Mavis I got him a new set of golf clubs and I told the assistant that as I
don't know a putter from a caddie he could expect a visit from my
husband to change every damn one of them. I approve of him playing
golf. While he's chasing that ridiculous little ball I know he's not
chasing anything else. He's fifty, and that's a dangerous age. Look at

Miriam's husband! Happily married for twenty years then he reaches fifty, and what happens? Goes off the rails for the first time in his married life with a young woman. Trying to be with it when he'd be far better off without it.

John, who is listening, reacts to this

That'll be George's trouble unless I keep an eye on him. He was giving you more than a friendly glance the other night. God! I'd love to soak my feet in ice-cold water.

Kay George was not looking at me like that.

Mavis Darling, of course he was. It wasn't so much you, dear, as his age. He has the urge to make the effort before the effort's too much for the urge. But, darling, don't think I mind about you, I don't.

Kay Thank you.

Mavis My dear, it's too ridiculous. Anyhow, George would bore you to tears. The poor darling bores me beyond endurance sometimes.

Kay I suppose it is barely possible that you drive him up the wall too.

Mavis That's not the remark of a true friend. It is very easy for a man to bore a woman, and they frequently do, poor darlings. After all, dear, you've had four affairs and each one finished because you got bored. I know that Graham, to mention one, was dreadfully upset at the time. Still, you are lucky, darling, you are free to chop and change your emotions. It must be very convenient. My feet are beginning to simmer down at last, thank God! Isn't it about time you got weaving with kettle and teapot?

Kay (*rising*) Yes, yes. (*She picks up a magazine from the coffee-table and tosses it to Mavis*) Amuse yourself, I won't be long. There's a lovely article in there on how to keep your husband by Marjory Proops.

Mavis I have yet to see a magazine for men with articles on how to keep your wife.

Mavis takes the magazine and proceeds to fan her feet with it. Kay enters the kitchenette and closes the door

John (*stiffly*) Charming, I must say!

Kay (*flinging her arms around him*) Darling, darling, that's Mavis. Bicarbonate of soda—remember?

John (*trying to release himself*) She's poison ivy to me.

Kay (*hanging on*) She is to me at this moment. (*She kisses him quickly*) Darling, please!

John Make her tea, for God's sake, otherwise she'll be popping in here to continue her revelations or to borrow a bowl to soak her damned feet.

Kay (*busy with kettle, cups, etc., throughout the following*) Darling, please, I'll get rid of her. I'll tell her I've got to go out.

John I can't understand why you opened the door in the first place.

Kay I thought it was the delivery boy with the drinks.

John He could have left them on the landing and that's where you should have left her.

Kay If you hadn't wasted so much time I wouldn't have been in a position to open the door.

John Perhaps it's just as well.

Kay Why?

John Your friend Mavis said quite a lot.

Kay Darling, please, Mavis talks a lot of nonsense. You heard what she said about George.

John And has he got my sympathy! But it wasn't what she said about George.

Kay What Mavis says . . .

Mavis Kay, darling!

Kay (*pushing John back and opening the door*) Yes?

Mavis Do you need any help?

Kay Of course not. It won't take a moment. You sit and rest your feet. (*She closes the door*)

Mavis Darling!

Kay Damn, damn, double damn! (*She opens the door*) Yes, darling?

Mavis Don't keep on closing the door, we can still talk.

Kay I always close the kitchenette door, it stops the cooking smells getting into the flat. (*She closes the door*)

Mavis I must say I have never smelt tea and surely to God you aren't cooking kippers!

Kay (*shouting*) I won't be a moment.

John For heaven's sake give that woman her bloody tea. I'm getting claustrophobia.

Kay Oh darling, I'm sorry. I'll get rid of her.

John And it's getting near four o'clock. Miss Adams will be wondering what's happened to me. I'm never late.

Kay Damn Miss Adams! If Mavis hadn't arrived, dictating to that woman would have been the last thing you'd have been thinking about.

John Stuck in this cell of little ease, it's all I'm thinking about now.

Kay What on earth made you come in here in the first place?

John It was a bolt-hole.

Kay What's the use of my being in the bedroom if you're going to bolt to the kitchen?

Mavis Kay, darling!

Kay Oh drop dead! (*She opens the door*) Yes, darling?

Mavis Have you got the wireless on in there?

Kay Yes, but I've switched it off now. I won't be a moment. (*She closes the door and then speaks in a hoarse whisper*) Darling, I love you and don't bolt from here. The only exit is through that window and I'm four floors up. (*She flings her arms around John and gives him a quick passionate kiss*) I'll get rid of her. (*She has now arranged the tray with all the accessories, including a plate of biscuits. She picks up the tray and goes into the lounge, closing the kitchenette door behind her*) There, I wasn't long, was I? Kettle will be boiling in a minute.

Mavis Good! I'm dying for a cup. Oooooh! My favourite biscuits. (*She takes one and starts eating*) I shouldn't really, I'm on a diet, but what the hell! I'm always on a diet. I can't understand it, I just put on weight regardless. If I eat a lettuce leaf it sinks to my bottom. I'll just have to face the fact that I'm fat—well, plump.

Kay Cuddlesome!

Mavis You say the nicest things, but nobody wants to cuddle me. You're the type they go for, God knows why. There's so much more fun in a fat girl, a never-ending field of exploration. These are nice biscuits, I think I'll have another.

Kay Do! By the way Mavis, I don't want to push you out, but I do have a date.

Mavis Really, darling, who with?

Kay Just a date. I was changing when you arrived.

Mavis Don't be so secretive, darling. Is it Graham?

Kay No, it isn't.

Mavis I just wondered, as you were out with him the other night. I thought he might be—er—on again.

Kay Two nights ago I had dinner with a Bishop, and he's not on either.

The kettle whistles, John goes to turn down the gas, remembers, and hastily withdraws his hand

Kettle's boiling. I won't be a moment.

Kay goes into the kitchenette and closes the door

John (*in a hoarse whisper*) Who's this Graham?

Kay (*busy with kettle and teapot, also speaking in a hoarse whisper*) Darling, an episode from my past.

John Then what's he doing in the present?

Kay (*delightedly*) How wonderful! You're jealous.

John I am not jealous! I've got claustrophobia, everybody's getting tea except me, it's getting on for four o'clock. I hate this goddamned kitchen—but I am *not* jealous!

Kay Sh! Sh!

John I repeat, I am not jealous. But if the past half an hour is a sample of what a love affair is like, Casanova must have been stark, raving mad! (*He points to the lounge*) And I don't like her, either!

Kay Darling, I'm so sorry.

Kay pours a little water from the kettle into the teapot

John And stop waving that damn pot under my nose. What on earth are you doing?

Kay Warming the pot. You must always warm the pot.

John Warming the . . .! Give it to me!

John takes a packet of tea bags and empties the lot in the pot

Kay Darling, you'll give her tannin poisoning.

John So?

Kay (*giggling and pouring more water into the pot*) Darling, I promise!

One cup and that's her lot. (*She looks into the pot*) As I think it will be! (*She takes the teapot and goes into the lounge*) Here's the tea.

Mavis By the way, I saw Angela the other day.

Kay (*busy pouring tea*) How was she? Her usual sweet, charming, two-faced self?

Mavis Angela was lunching last week at the Padonni. Lovely little place, she said. Food was so good. Very cosy and intimate.

Kay I hope she enjoyed herself.

Mavis I believe she did. Have you been there, darling?

Kay You know damn well I have, otherwise you would never have mentioned it.

Mavis Who was he?

Kay A friend of mine.

Mavis Angela said he was quite old.

John reacts

Kay Angela is so young that anyone over thirty is in the sere and yellow.

Mavis But compared with Graham Angela said he looked very old. She was quite surprised. She also said he looked very staid, rather like a church deacon.

John reacts

Kay Considering that Angela has only been to church twice, her christening and her wedding, her knowledge of church deacons is somewhat limited.

Mavis Darling, you know Angela. As I said to her, you can't go by looks. A lot of these church people have hidden fires. I mean, look at the size of some of their families. He hasn't ecclesiastical connections, has he?

Kay (*giggling*) He's shown no sign of them.

Mavis I knew that Angela was exaggerating. Darling, you must bring him to dinner one night. We'd love to meet him. Just the four of us.

Kay For Angela's benefit I'll get him to say grace.

Mavis Darling, you are being just the teeny bit sarcastic. Could I have a drop more tea? Then I really must go.

Kay I'm afraid you'll have to.

Kay picks up the teapot to pour

Mavis Darling, I know I don't like weak tea, but this is ridiculous! Weaken it for God's sake!

Kay Oh, sorry!

Kay goes into the kitchen

John Now what?

Kay More hot water.

John I'd like to strangle that bitch and sweet Angela.

Kay (*giggling*) Sh! darling, she'll hear you, and that doesn't sound a bit deacon like.

John And if you think I'm going there to dinner . . .

Kay flings her arms around his neck and kisses him. She then proceeds to pour the water from the kettle into the teapot. Meanwhile Mavis rises and moves over to the windows and looks out. Suddenly she sees John's bowler hat on the window-seat and picks it up. She gazes at it aghast, and then looks quickly at the closed bedroom door. She then hurries to the armchair and hastily puts on her shoes, grabs her handbag, and hurriedly goes to the front door. She suddenly realizes that she is still holding the bowler hat. She turns to replace it on the window-seat when Kay enters the lounge. Mavis stands with the hat held in front of her

Mavis (*in a hoarse whisper*) Darling, I didn't know, I didn't guess. But I should have done with you dressed like that. Is he ...? (*She gestures towards the bedroom*)

Kay (*also in a hoarse whisper*) Yes!

Mavis Oh my God! Could he have heard us?

Kay I shouldn't be surprised.

Mavis Don't bring him to dinner. I couldn't face him.

Kay I won't.

Mavis He must be going mad. Darling, I'm so sorry. Tell him I'm sorry. But it's not my fault. Why did you open the door to me?

Kay I thought you were the delivery boy with the drinks.

Mavis You couldn't be that thirsty. I'm going. I'll ring you tomorrow.

Mavis turns and opens the front door

Kay Mavis!

Mavis (*turning*) What?

Kay George is bound to ask questions if you go home holding a bowler hat.

Mavis What? (*Suddenly she realizes and throws the hat to Kay, who catches it*) Kay! (*She gestures violently towards the bedroom door*) Carry on, darling! I'm sorry! Oh my God!

Mavis hurriedly exits, closing the front door

Kay (*going off into peals of laughter*) Darling, darling, come out of your little bolt-hole!

John (*poking his head out of the kitchenette*) Has that purveyor of scandal gone?

Kay Completely and utterly routed.

Kay goes to John and goes to put her arms around him, then realizes that she has a teapot in one hand and a bowler hat in the other

Pardon me! Oh, to hell with it!

Kay puts her arms around John and kisses him passionately

John (*breaking away*) It's nearly four o'clock. I must go. Miss Adams w be waiting and ...

Kay (*hanging on*) I swear that woman has a hold over you.

John But she'll be waiting for my letters, and I'm never late.

Kay (*kissing him between words*) And I'm waiting, too, and I'm getting
   impatient.
John Oh, darling ...

*Kay, still with hands full, slips her arm through John's and starts to lead
him towards the bedroom. At that moment, the telephone starts to ring
and a second or so later there is a ringing at the front door*

   (*Shouting*) Damn and blast everything!! One might as well make love
   in the middle of Waterloo Station.
Kay Darling, please!
John (*furiously*) It's no damn good. Answer that phone it might be
   Graham!

John snatches his hat from Kay and goes to the front door and pulls it open

   Standing there is a Delivery Boy with a basket of bottles

Boy Are you Mr Brent?
John No! I'm a bloody church deacon!

John brushes furiously past the Boy as—

                    the CURTAIN *quickly falls*

ACT II

SCENE 1

The same. An early afternoon in October

Again the only radical alteration in the scene is the vase of flowers on the telephone-table. It is now filled with chrysanthemums

When the CURTAIN *rises, John is seated leaning back on the couch. Kay is just lifting a tray of used plates from the coffee-table. Kay is relaxed, and from the expression on her face—amused. John however, is looking frigid and irritable. It is noticeable now and throughout the scene that he is now very much at home in the flat*

Kay (*standing holding the tray*) Though I say so myself I thought that was a superb spaghetti bolognese I prepared.

John (*shortly*) Very nice.

Kay (*sweetly*) Thank you, I'm *so* glad you enjoyed it. And the Camembert was to your liking?

John You know it was.

Kay You couldn't have done better at Padonni's. I'll get the coffee.

Kay takes the tray to the kitchenette. The coffee percolator is bubbling on the stove. She places the tray on the sink then pours the coffee from the percolator into the coffee-pot which is on a tray with cups, etc. She then brings the coffee-tray into the lounge and places it in the centre of the coffee-table and seats herself on the opposite end of the sofa to John

Coffee! (*She lights a cigarette*) Brandy?

John (*still very short*) Please.

Kay rises, moves to the drinks cabinet and takes out a bottle of brandy. She then turns and surveys John's back for a moment or two

Kay I like mine black, as you know.

John Oh!

John pours out two cups of coffee and almost throws the sugar into them while Kay watches him. She then pours two glasses of brandy and brings them back to the sofa and hands one to John. She reseats herself in her former position

Kay (*cheerfully raising her glass*) Happy days and happier nights as my ex was fond of saying.

John They probably have been. (*He gulps his brandy*)

Kay They haven't been exactly devoid of interest.

John You don't have to tell me that.

Kay Then I won't waste my breath.

John rises abruptly and goes to the drinks cabinet and pours himself another brandy. At the same time Kay picks up a newspaper from the telephone-table and a pencil and commences to do the crossword puzzle. John remains at the cabinet with his drink in his hand

John I've been away a week.

Kay (*intent on the crossword*) "Towards the sunset on a beautiful horse." Four words! Four, two, five, four.

John What *are* you doing?

Kay A crossword puzzle.

John I said I've been away a week.

Kay I know. Brighton! Did you have a good time?

John I didn't go for a good time.

Kay Too bad! One usually goes to Brighton for one thing.

John You know very well I went there for a business conference. (*Pompously*) The Public Libraries Conference Exhibition.

Kay (*looking up from her crossword*) Really! Pick up any good pornographic books you could recommend? (*Back to the crossword*) "Towards the sunset on a beautiful horse."

John I sent you a postcard and phoned you five times. Five!

Kay And only got me twice, but thanks for the postcard.

John And what does that prove?

Kay That Brighton pier looks like any other pier and I was out three times. Consequently you have been showing your icy disapproval ever since you arrived.

John I have not!

Kay Then what have you been doing?

John does not answer, and after a moment starts to do his perambulating round the room

"Towards the sunset on a beautiful horse." Now the sun sinks in the west.

John Force of habit, it's been doing it for years. Must you do that damned crossword when I'm talking to you?

Kay In your present mood—yes! Now what's a horse?

John A solid-hoofed quadruped!

Kay It doesn't say that here, just a beautiful horse. You make it sound like a pre-historic monster. Towards the sunset on a beautiful solid-hoofed quadruped!

John For God's sake stop trying to be funny!

Kay You're not even trying, and there's nothing funny about this crossword. Listen to this! "Lazy workers"—four words. Six, two, three, five. Got it! (*Writing*) Lilies of the field! (*To John*) Lazy workers . . .

John They toil not neither do they spin! Now have you finished apart from that horse?

Kay Finished? That's the only one I've got so far. "Towards the sunset . . ."

John For God's sake let's be done with that damned horse! (*He flings himself on the sofa and practically snatches the paper from Kay*)
Kay Thank you! It's one across.
John (*studying it for a moment*) The answer's obvious. (*He hands the paper back to Kay*)
Kay Well, what is it?
John You're doing the crossword, not me!
Kay You wanted to be done with the damned horse, so what is it?

John picks up his glass and sips his brandy

Don't sit there so smug and damned complacent. What is it? Answer me!
John In your present mood—no!

Kay opens her mouth to retort furiously—then suddenly giggles

Kay Please tell me why somebody is going towards the sunset on a beautiful horse?
John (*very superior*) They are going west on super mare. Weston-super-Mare. It's in Somerset.
Kay I know *that*! (*Scribbling furiously*) Of course that's the answer. I'm an idiot. You are clever.
John Having at last settled the destination of that horse can you now forget that damned crossword?
Kay (*smiling*) I suppose I can finish it later.
John Much later?
Kay That depends.
John On what?
Kay On you.

John suddenly leans forward and puts his arms around Kay and kisses her passionately. Kay's hands, however, just rest on his shoulders and the paper is still in her hand. John moves from her mouth and kissing her cheek moves, still kissing, onto her neck and shoulder. Kay holds the paper over his shoulder and reads from it

"For I have need of many somethings
  To move the heavens to smile upon my state,
  Which, well thou know'st, is cross and full of sin."

John, his head still buried in her neck, stops kissing. There is a pause, then he slowly raises his head

John *Pardon?*
Kay (*withdrawing*) If Weston-super-Mare is right—and I'm sure it is— that something begins with an "O" and it's got seven letters. It's a quotation.
John (*violently*) I don't believe it!!
Kay It's true! It says it's from *Romeo and Juliet*. I hate quotations. The only ones I readily recognize from Shakespeare are "Friends, Romans, Countrymen", and "To be or not to be".

John That's the very one I'm thinking of at the moment. (*He angrily picks up his glass and drains it*)

Kay (*ignoring the inference and tapping the paper with her pencil*) They've got a new man doing these now. As soon as you get used to one man's way of doing things, they change him. You can always tell.

John You certainly can, and not only in crosswords. (*He angrily moves across to the drinks cabinet*)

Kay Do have another brandy if it will make you feel better.

John Thank you. (*He pours himself one*) But I doubt whether I shall feel better.

Kay Never mind, have another and feel a damn sight worse. Meanwhile, I'll concentrate on what Juliet needs. (*She goes back to the paper*) This man's quotation mad! Listen to this one! "To him the pleasure of love is in loving." Two words. Two and thirteen. Thirteen!! That could be anybody.

John (*still by the cabinet*) You should know.

Kay Meaning?

John Do I have to spell it out?

Kay With thirteen letters—definitely yes! I can probably manage the other two.

John I didn't mean the crossword.

Kay Oh, and I was hoping you were going to be frightfully clever like you were with Weston-super-Mare.

John Well, I'm not!

Kay (*smiling and shaking her head*) No, my dear, you're not being very clever at all.

John And what's that supposed to mean?

Kay (*laughing and flinging the paper down*) Darling, you're behaving like an idiot.

John (*stiffly*) Thank you!

Kay (*picking up her glass*) And don't stand there swigging all the brandy—give me some, too.

John, slightly bewildered, comes and takes her glass, goes back to the cabinet and pours brandy into it. He then returns and hands her the glass

Well, bring your glass as well or are you permanently parked at the bar?

John goes to the cabinet, collects his glass, returns and sits

That's better! (*Cheerfully*) Cheers!

John (*dignifiedly*) Your health! How am I behaving like an idiot?

Kay Very successfully.

John Was I behaving like an idiot when I kissed you a few moments ago?

Kay Slightly—yes!

John Slightly—yes?

Kay Yes, it was nice, but I don't consider the answer to a crossword clue excuses your sheer bloody-mindedness since you arrived. And I don't think Weston-super-Mare, however clever, justifies the reward of hopping between the sheets with you.

John (*outraged*) I never intended that!

Kay (*knowing that he did*) Good, that's settled then. Now we can really be nice and cosy. (*She picks up the paper again*) "For I have need of many somethings". Now if I get that something that will give me one of the thirteen letters of that man's name. Two and thirteen. If the first word has only two letters he must obviously be French.

Kay studies her crossword, sucking her pencil. There is a pause

John (*eventually rising and perambulating again*) I've been away a week. A week! And what do I come back to?

Kay Me and spaghetti bolognese.

John Do you realize that this is the first time since we met that we've been parted for any length of time? I've missed you! You don't realize how much.

Kay And I've missed you, too.

John suddenly comes forward, leans over the sofa, and kisses Kay passionately

John (*after an interval*) Is that bloody-mindedness?
Kay No! Very sexy!

John kisses her passionately again

John Still sexy?
Kay Mm!! More so!
John Well then—well . . .

John casually moves across to Kay's bedroom and exits

Kay looks up with a smile and resumes her crossword

Kay "—which, well thou know'st, is cross and full of sin." Sin! Full of sin! She needs—needs . . . (*She gives a delighted cry*) Got it! I've remembered. Darling, where are you?
John (*off*) Where do you think I am?
Kay I know what Juliet needed.

John comes out of the bedroom, minus his jacket, and leans against the door

John Romeo?
Kay Orisons. (*Writing*) I'm glad I remembered that. Now that gives an "O" in the middle of that Frenchman's name who had a one-track mind about love.
John He could be English! They enjoy a bit of pleasure too, y'know! It isn't the prerogative of the French.

John turns and goes into the bedroom again

Kay gives a smile, puts down her paper, takes a cigarette from the box and lights it. She curls up on the sofa and smokes contentedly

John reappears, this time minus his waistcoat, tie, and with his shirt unbuttoned

Kay (*surveying him*) What are you doing, the dance of the seven veils?

John What do you think I'm doing?

Kay It's a funny time for a bath, especially after lunch.

John I'm not undressing for a bath! It's because—because.

Kay Well then, darling, if you feel more comfortable like that, then make yourself at home. But don't catch cold. (*She picks up her crossword again and studies it*)

John You're evidently not interested.

Kay Darling, you look lovely.

John But not as lovely as some you could possibly mention—like Graham for instance!

John turns furiously and goes back into the bedroom and slams the door

Kay carries on with her crossword and fills in a couple of clues

John re-enters, now once again fully clothed, and seats himself violently on the sofa and folds his arms

Kay looks up and surveys him again

Kay Your tie's crooked.

John (*savagely straightening it*) Satisfied?

Kay Much better! While you've been dashing in and out of my bedroom I've filled in two more clues. Apart from the "O" that Frenchman has a "C" and an "A". It's a blank, "O", "C", then bank, blank, blank . . .

John Damn that crossword and to hell with that bloody Frenchman! I'm going to have another drink!

Kay You'll get plastered.

John There doesn't seem to be much else to do.

John rises, goes to the drink cabinet and pours himself another brandy

Kay Why? What had you in mind?

John (*amazed*) What had I in mind? I've been away a week and—

Kay —you phoned me five times and I was out for three of them, and this is what it's all about! What did you expect me to do for a week? Sit on my bottom by the telephone?

John (*shouting*) Well, what did you do?

Kay At last! At long last!

John At last what?

Kay The inquisition! You've been bloody-minded since you arrived and at last you've come out with it. No more veiled references, no more innuendoes, just a plain what have you been up to while I've been away? You've been longing to ask but you wanted to choose your own moment —and I know when that would have been. After we'd been in bed for an hour, *then* the questions and innuendoes would have come. But only afterwards! Now I'll save you the bother. Have you ever been to an orgy?

John A what?

Kay An orgy! You know what they are! Wild revels, debaucheries!

John (*horror-struck*) Good God, no! (*Even more horror-struck*) Why, have you?

Kay Yes!

John When?

Kay Three times last week! I'm worn out! But now I've confessed before-hand. You know what I've been up to—so now we can hop into bed if you still feel inclined!

John (*still horror-struck*) You're joking!

Kay suddenly bursts into peals of laughter

Kay Darling, your face is a study!

John I'm glad you find it amusing.

Kay I do! I wouldn't even know where to find an orgy even if I wanted one. I'm sure they don't advertise in "Yellow Pages"!

John A stupid joke still doesn't explain . . .

Kay You're getting jealous, that's your trouble, darling. You've shown a distinct tendency in that direction recently, and I don't like it.

John (*stiffly*) I wasn't aware of it.

Kay Oh darling, come off it, you are! I admit I like a little jealousy, I wouldn't be a woman if I didn't; but only a little because it flatters and shows love. But too much . . . Ugh! That shows mistrust. Now, I've been out three times, but that isn't a crime.

John With Graham, no doubt!

Kay See what I mean? There you go again! Graham is now just a friend. *Friend*—period! Let's clear the air, shall we? I'm under no obligation to, but I will. I'm a free agent. I go where I like, see whom I like, and do as I like—but that doesn't mean a ceaseless round of bed-hopping.

John Kay!!

Kay That's what you think and it doesn't mean that at all. One night I went to the theatre with Mavis, the other night I went to the cinema—alone! And the other night I went out to dinner with—wait for it—Graham! And it was a perfect bore.

John I find that difficult to believe.

Kay Well, it was! He phoned me up and asked me out to dinner, and I thought it was for the sheer pleasure of my company, which incidentally, was all he was going to get.

John And he only wanted the pleasure of your company?

Kay Not really! He's now madly infatuated with a young lady called Cynthia. Why is it when a person gets like that they can't stop talking about their adored? I had her for the entire evening, her virtues, her brains, her wit, all of which were wonderful. I tried to stop the flow by even dragging Harold Wilson into the conversation. I should have chosen Enoch Powell. Her father's name was Harold and he was off again. So you see, darling, he only took me out to dinner to talk about her.

John So what did you do?

Kay Ordered the most expensive items on the menu. I thought I deserved some reward.

John I can sympathize with Graham.

Kay Why?

John Because I know how he feels about Cynthia. I want to tell the whole world about you—but I can't!

Kay Now that's nice, darling.

John (*simply*) I'm sorry, my dear, I'm a fool!

Kay I'm afraid you are.

John But I love you so much—so very much.

Kay suddenly crosses to him, puts her arms around him, and they kiss passionately

Better?

Kay Much, much better.

John Well then . . .

John moves across to the bedroom, looks back at Kay, and exits

She moves to follow, then goes to the sofa and sits down again

John (*after a moment; off*) Darling!

Kay still sits

John enters again, once more minus his coat, waistcoat, tie, and his shirt is unbuttoned

John Kay . . . (*He sees her sitting there*) Oh my God, now what?

Kay Just one question, darling.

John Make it quick!

Kay You know you phoned me five times and only got me twice.

John But we've been over that, darling.

Kay And you know how bloody-minded you were.

John (*in despair*) Dearest, I've said I was sorry.

Kay Well, I phoned *you* on two evenings.

John You phoned me twice?

Kay Yes, and you were out each time, and *I* haven't said a word. Now what does that prove?

John (*coming over and kissing her*) That you don't expect me to sit on my bottom by the telephone.

Kay bursts out laughing, and he puts an arm around her and leads her to the bedroom

Kay Now to prove the pleasure of love is in loving.

They reach the bedroom door

John Said, incidentally, by a gentleman named La Rochefoucauld.

Kay You beast! You knew all the time! (*She leaves him and rushes back to the sofa and picks up paper and pencil*)

John (*in despair*) Oh no!!

John leans his head in his arms at the door post as—

the CURTAIN *quickly falls*

SCENE 2

The same. An afternoon in late December

Again the only radical alteration in the room is the fact that the vase usually full of flowers is no longer there

When the CURTAIN *rises the stage is fairly dark. It is about three o'clock in the afternoon. The sky is grey and heavy and one can see the lights in the flats across the square. After a moment the sound of a key in the lock of the front door, it opens, and light streams in from the landing. John is seen silhouetted in the doorway. He switches on the lights from the switch by the door and the room is lit by a cosy glow. He enters closing the front door, and puts the key in his trouser pocket. He is dressed in a heavy overcoat and wears his usual bowler hat and carries an umbrella*

John Kay! (*He listens for a moment*) Damn!

He moves across to the bedroom and looks inside. He comes out and takes off his hat and overcoat and lays them on the window-seat and places his umbrella there also. He then goes across to the drinks cabinet and takes out a bottle of whisky and a glass and pours himself a drink. He then moves across to the couch and is about to sit down when there is a ring at the front door-bell. He pauses irresolute, then sits down and sips his drink. After a moment the ring is repeated. Suddenly, with an air of determination, he places his glass on the telephone-table and goes to the front door and opens it wide

   He reveals a Visitor standing there. He is about forty-five, immaculately dressed, good-looking, with rather a sardonic face that betokens an impish sense of humour

Visitor (*with cheerful casualness*) Oh, hallo!
John (*after a moment*) Yes?
Visitor Is Kay there?
John No she isn't!
Visitor Will she be long?
John I've no idea.
Visitor Oh! Do you know where she is?
John I don't know that either.
Visitor This is a damn nuisance. I was hoping to see her.

John eyes the Visitor

John (*suspiciously*) Oh, were you! Was Mrs Brent expecting you?
Visitor (*amused*) I wouldn't know. But I adore giving pleasant surprises. Don't you? I always think . . .
John Who are you?

The Visitor passes John and enters the flat. John is taken by surprise

   (*Angrily*) Where the devil do you think you're going?

Visitor (*turning*) Eh? Nowhere, just here!

John This is Mrs Brent's flat.

Visitor I know that! If you remember I asked for her, and . . .

John I strongly object to perfect strangers pushing in.

Visitor Far from perfect I assure you, and I didn't push I just walked in.

John Then just walk out again.

Visitor Why?

John Well, I don't know you! You could be anybody!

Visitor I don't know you either, but I don't object to you.

John I should damn well hope not. Now will you please get out.

Visitor Then why object to me?

John (*pompously*) Because I am here by Mrs Brent's invitation. (*Moving down and eyeing the Visitor suspiciously*) Why are you here?

Visitor My dear fellow, I've told you. To see Kay.

John Well, I've told you she isn't here and I have no idea when she'll be back. You could leave a message.

Visitor True!

John Then give it to me.

Visitor But it's terribly private and confidential.

John (*abruptly*) Oh!!

Visitor So you see . . .

John Then you'll have to telephone her. (*He gestures to the still open front door*) So, do you mind . . .?

Visitor Telephone? With something private and confidential? My dear chap, have you ever had a crossed line? The things one hears . . .

John I don't! I always replace the receiver.

Visitor Ah! Then you don't have an insatiable curiosity.

John Well, if you can't leave the message with me . . . (*He goes back to the front door*) Good-bye!

Visitor Why, are you going? Oh really, please don't leave on my account.

John I'm not going—you are!

The Visitor gracefully sits in an armchair and crosses his legs

What the hell do you think you're doing?

Visitor Sitting down!

John (*angrily; still at the door*) Then I should stand up again! It might be quite an hour or so before she returns—perhaps longer—so you're wasting your time. Good afternoon!

Visitor (*gently*) Then why are you waiting?

John Because—because . . .

Visitor (*wagging a finger at John*) You know, old man, I'm getting very suspicious of you.

John What!! (*He slams the front door*) Suspicious of me? Don't be so damned impertinent!

Visitor I've every right to be suspicious. (*Rising and counting his remarks on his fingers*) One, you don't know where Kay is. Two, you've no idea when she'll be back. Three, if you are here at her invitation why don't you know the answers to questions one and two—and why do you still

wait even though it may be hours? Four, you object to my coming in.
And lastly, five, you're too damned anxious to get rid of me. (*Sharply*)
Do you know what I think? I think you're a burglar!

John (*outraged*) A burglar!!! How dare you! I'll ...

Visitor Don't move! Have you ransacked her bedroom? She keeps her
jewellery in there.

The Visitor goes straight into the bedroom

John stands stupeified

A moment later the Visitor reappears out of the bathroom door

I merely checked the bathroom. (*Pointing to the kitchenette*) Nothing
of value in the kitchen. (*Surveying the room*) I seem to have arrived in
the nick of time.

John What the devil do you mean?

Visitor (*pointing to John's whisky-glass on the telephone-table*) Obviously
after a drink you were about to ransack the flat.

John Now look here, I've stood about as much from you ...

Visitor Being an honest, God-fearing citizen, I rang the bell. A perfect
stranger opens the door. He can't tell me where the occupant of the flat
is, when she'll be back, makes every effort to keep me out, and says she
invited him. If Kay isn't here, how did you get in?

John With a key! How else would I get in?

Visitor A skeleton key, obviously! However, if you are an honest, upright,
God fearing citizen as I am, you will have no objection to my calling
the police and explaining the situation to them.

John What!! You can't call the police!

Visitor Why not? Have you got a record?

John Of course I haven't got a record, you fool.

The Visitor goes to the telephone and picks up the receiver

What the hell are you doing now?

Visitor Dialling nine-nine-nine.

John (*rushing forward and clamping his hand down on the telephone*)
Don't be a bloody fool! You can't bring the police here.

Visitor Why not? My conscience is clear. Now will you take your hand
away and let me do my duty.

John Do you think Mrs Brent—Kay—would want the police here? Are
you mad? I'm a friend of hers.

Visitor Under the circumstances I don't think she'd object, and I don't
think you should either. Kay would be very grateful that we had her
interest at heart. And apart from that the police would be thrilled.
They're very keen on this crime prevention lark. If you see anything
suspicious—ring the police. It is the duty of every honest citizen. And
this is me doing my duty. In any case, I've always longed to dial nine-
nine-nine, and say dramatically—police!

John (*shouting*) Will you please stop playing the fool!

Visitor I am not playing the fool. This light-hearted banter of mine really covers a quaking heart. I'm petrified, I am really. I'm quite a coward, you know. I've never met a criminal . . .

John God damn it! Do I look like a criminal?

Visitor If one knew what a criminal looked like we wouldn't need a police force.

John Look at me! I'm a respectable businessman!

Visitor So was Crippen, and look what happened to him! But your conscience is clear?

John God Almighty, of course it is.

Visitor Good! Then you'll certainly have no objection to my ringing the police. You can face Dixon, or Barlow, or whoever they send along, with your head held high. You've nothing to worry about.

John This is ridiculous . . .

Visitor I hope, for your sake, they send Sergeant Dixon. He's nice and understanding. God help you if Barlow comes. He'd even make the Pope feel guilty.

John (*taking out his handkerchief and mopping his brow*) Now look here! I tell you I'm a friend of Mrs Brent's.

Visitor (*replacing the telephone receiver*) So you say! All right, we'll forget the police for the moment. You've got to admit, old man, I have every right to be suspicious. However, we will try and straighten things out. What's your name?

John John Browne, blast you!

The Visitor looks at him and lifts the receiver again

What the blazes are you doing now?

Visitor (*with his finger poised over the dial*) I gave you a chance, old man, but really—John Browne!

John (*shouting*) I am John Browne! God damn it, I can't help it if my father's name was Browne.

Visitor (*with his finger still poised*) I bet at this moment you wish your mother had married someone else.

John At this moment I wish to God your mother had never been born! My name is Browne! (*He takes out his wallet and extracts his driving licence*) Look! (*He tosses it to the Visitor*) Now do you believe me?

Visitor (*looking at it*) Oh, Browne with an "e"! That seems genuine enough. Of course, it might have been stolen from the last place you ransacked. (*He flicks a page*) Ah-ha! You have got a record! Your licence has been endorsed for speeding! (*He tosses it back to John*) O.K.! So you are John Browne.

John Now are you completely and utterly satisfied?

Visitor Not quite. How did you get in?

John I told you I have a key. (*He puts his hand in his trouser pocket and pulls it out*) Here!

The Visitor takes the key and moves across to the front door, opens it, inserts key in lock and turns it

Visitor Just checking. You could have given me any key.

The Visitor closes door again and gives the key back to John

John Now I hope you are thoroughly satisfied and that you feel you have done your duty as an honest, upright citizen!

Visitor I feel very noble and virtuous. It's a lovely feeling.

John I'm glad you are enjoying it. I'm sure you very rarely experience *those* feelings!

Visitor Well, I certainly can't claim to be virtuous, very few of us can. But you too could have enjoyed a certain complacency if you had let me send for the police. Think how smug you would have felt! Your innocence vindicated, and I would have slunk out the door with my head bowed in shame.

John You still can, you know the way out!

Visitor Why didn't you let me send for the police?

John Just as well for you I didn't. It would have made you look ridiculous.

Visitor I couldn't imagine you foregoing that pleasure. No, I think it's just as well for *you* I didn't.

John What do you mean?

Visitor (*sinking into an armchair and sticking his feet out*) Thoroughly at home, drinking the whisky, has the key of the flat!

John And what business is that of yours?

Visitor I could be very jealous.

John Jealous! What do you mean—jealous?

Visitor Oh, just jealous. But I'm just wondering.

John Wondering what?

Visitor If there is a Mrs Browne!

John reacts

Ah-ha! Bull's eye! My dear fellow, no wonder you didn't want any dealings with the police. How very awkward explaining to Mrs B. about the other Mrs B! You're quite busy with your "Bs", aren't you! Actually, you needn't have worried. Our police are wonderful. They are the soul of discretion.

John angrily moves across to the drinks cabinet, pours himself some more whisky, and drinks

But you are not the soul of hospitality. You might say—have a drink, old man!

John (*starting to walk moodily around*) Help yourself. I'm sure you've done so many times before.

Visitor (*rising*) Thanks, I will! (*He goes across and helps himself to whisky*) Why do you say I have helped myself before?

John Pretty obvious, isn't it! You know your way round the flat.

Visitor Well, it isn't exactly like Buckingham Palace! Now one might get lost there.

John You found your way to the bedroom quick enough!

The Visitor gives John a shrewd look

Who are you, anyway? You've gone to great lengths to establish my presence here.

Visitor My dear fellow, I'm a friend of Kay's, the same as you.

John (*sharply*) The same as me? What do you mean, the same as me?

Visitor Well, aren't you a friend? That's what you led me to believe.

John (*shortly*) Yes!

Visitor Now isn't that nice. We're all friends together.

John (*savagely*) If we sit here much longer probably a few more friends will turn up!

Visitor My word! Wouldn't Kay be surprised!

John I bet she would! You seem to know Kay very well.

Visitor As well as you, probably, old man!

John looks at the Visitor sharply, but he is drinking his whisky

Friendly person, our Kay!

John Too damn friendly!

Visitor What's wrong in that? But when I say friendly—a wide circle of acquaintances—yes, but close friends, such as you and I . . .

John Probably an even wider circle.

Visitor She's been a great comfort to me many a time.

John I'm sure she has.

Visitor (*earnestly*) Oh, she has! I always feel with Kay that she understands me.

John Have you come round to be comforted now?

Visitor No, I just dropped in on the off chance—of seeing her. In any case, old man, you were here first and I was here last.

John But many that are first shall be last; and the last shall be first.

Visitor Matthew nineteen, verse thirty. How very apt!

John But not on this occasion.

Visitor Y'know, I'm beginning to get the impression that you don't like me or my company.

John That is an understatement.

Visitor Now that upsets me! It really does! I admit we had a little misunderstanding earlier on, but my fault entirely. I was suspicious, and I feel that unfounded suspicions are unforgiveable.

John And I'm damn sure mine aren't! You wanted to leave a message, very private and confidential! Since I can't obviously take it, and the G.P.O. is a mass of crossed lines—

Visitor —and Kay, according to you, may not be back for hours . . . (*Snapping his fingers*) I could leave a note! Now why didn't I think of that before!

John Why didn't you! Well, carry on! I'm sure you know where the note-paper is kept, you know where everything else is.

Visitor Notepaper! Writing-desk. Paper, top left-hand shelf, envelopes underneath. Stamps, if required, centre shelf.

The Visitor moves across to the writing-desk, opens it and sits down. John standing near, tries to look without appearing to do so at where the notepaper is kept. The Visitor extracts a sheet with a flourish and looks at John

See! Just as I said! (*He takes his pen from his pocket and commences to write. After a moment he stops and turns to John*) Oh, I do beg your pardon! Please excuse me!

The Visitor resumes his writing and John turns and goes to the drinks cabinet again. He pours himself some more whisky. He stands there moodily drinking it and casting glances at the Visitor's back. Suddenly he bangs his fist violently on top of the cabinet. The Visitor swings round

Don't do that, old man! You made me jump! (*He looks at his letter*) I knew it! You made me do a squiggle. (*He resumes his letter*)

John starts to move moodily around the room, drinking his whisky, and casting frequent glances at the Visitor. The Visitor folds his letter, puts it in an envelope and scribbles on it. Then he props it up inside the desk, closes the desk, and rises

There all done! I presume you will be waiting here for Kay?

John (*definitely*) I will!

Visitor I thought you might. Good. Do please tell her there's a letter in the desk will you?

John (*curtly*) Yes!

Visitor Thank you so much, old chap! Good heavens, it's nearly three-thirty. I really must go. It's been so nice meeting you. We've had so much fun, haven't we! Well, cheerio, old boy!

The Visitor goes to the front door and opens it

John I'd like to punch you on the nose!

Visitor Good God! What for?

John (*turning away*) I'd just like to, that's all.

Visitor Now that's not nice at all. I don't see why you should be jealous of me. I'm not jealous of you.

John swings round

But then, I'm broad-minded, apart from having a beautiful nature. I forgive you. Please don't bother to see me out. Oh by the way, please give Kay my love.

John I'm sure you're quite capable of doing that yourself.

Visitor Yes, of course—next time I see her! Good-bye!

The Visitor exits, closing the door behind him

John takes a step towards the door, then turns and flings himself down on the couch. After a moment he gets up and wanders moodily around. He eyes the desk and moves over to it, then abruptly turns away, and sits in an armchair. He drinks, then as if drawn, his head turns towards the desk again. He rises and goes to it, and his hand reaches out to the lid. He pulls it open about six inches—then suddenly slams it too. He turns away and goes across to the drink cabinet again, gulps down the last of his drink, and slams the glass down. He stands for a moment undecided, then making a sudden decision he goes to the telephone and dials

John (*on the telephone*) Oh, Miss Adams ... I'll be back earlier than I anticipated—in fact, I'm on my way now ... Tailor? What do you mean, tailor? ... Did I? Oh yes, of course, I'm at the tailor's now. Mr Cresswell, the fitter, isn't here. He's ill, very ill! So I'm coming back to the office. Good-bye! (*He replaces the receiver and then goes to the window-seat and picks up his overcoat*)

At this moment the front door opens and Kay comes in. She turns to close the door and sees John

Kay (*surprised*) Hallo, what are you doing here?
John (*shortly*) Waiting for you, of course!
Kay And what's wrong with you, laughing-boy? I didn't know you were coming this afternoon. Been waiting long?
John Long enough.
Kay I've been out to lunch and got held up. (*She moves into the bedroom and her voice carries on*) Taxi was hours, literally hours in a hold-up. Every damn car in London seemed to have converged on Piccadilly. And, as usual, some idiot had left the gate open in the lift and I had to climb up. (*She comes out of the bedroom*) Infuriating! It went sailing down as I came panting up.

Kay looks at John, who is gazing stonily in front of him

Let joy be unconfined. Have some whisky and cheer yourself up.
John I've had some.
Kay (*seeing the whisky bottle*) You've knocked a hole in that lot, and I can't say it's cheered you up.

Kay moves towards John to kiss him and he abruptly turns away. Kay gives him an amused look then turns and goes to the couch, steps on it, sits on the arm, and surveys him

(*After a pause*) It's quite cold out.

John is silent

But not as cold as yesterday.

John makes no reply

I see in this morning's paper that the Prime Minister hopes to go to Chequers this week-end.

John turns and gazes out of the window

Oh, you evidently don't care where he goes.

Again no reaction from John

In about half a minute, perhaps less, I shall move to the whisky bottle, pick it up, and crown you with it, and to hell with the waste. (*A brief pause*) Answer me—you—you ...

Kay picks up a cushion and throws it at John. He catches it and throws it on the window-seat

John You weren't expecting me today, were you?
Kay No, I wasn't, not today.
John I'm damn sure you weren't!

Kay rises and stands on the couch, arms akimbo

Kay Right! Let's have a lovely, flaming row!
John I never row.
Kay No, you're like a bottle of wine, you ferment.
John Thank you.
Kay And you become a martyr, and I can't stand martyrs. They turn the other cheek.
John And what's wrong with that?
Kay (*jumping off the couch*) They aren't being good and pious. They know they are just being damned smug and infuriating to drive the other person nuts! So what is it, Saint John?
John Don't call me Saint John.
Kay On second thoughts that's hardly applicable. You never wore your halo on Monday afternoon.
John And I'm quite certain you never wore yours at lunch time. Who was it? Charles, Victor, Henry, Graham . . .?
Kay Oh, so this is going to be a flaming row after all. So that's it! I had the audacity to go out to lunch.
John And what were you coming back to?
Kay A dose of bismuth, it gave me indigestion. And after five minutes of you it's a damn sight worse. Pardon me while I relieve it. (*She turns and goes into the bathroom, leaving the door open, and her voice carries on*) I know this mood. I've got them all numbered. Number one is the obvious one. That was the mood you were in on Monday. Number two is the inquisitive—what have you been doing since I saw you last don't tell me I can guess mood. And number three—(*she comes out of the bathroom carrying a glass containing white liquid*)—is the present one. Downright bloody suspicious. Cheers! (*She raises her glass and drains it*) I hate the stuff but it does do the trick.
John (*icily*) I am sure the lunch was worth a little indigestion.
Kay The way I get indigestion no lunch is worth it. (*She returns to the bathroom to leave the glass*)
John From personal experience I find that hard to believe.
Kay (*entering from the bathroom*) My smiling face hid a burning heart. Now stop fencing, John, and come to the point quick.
John I see no sense in wasting my precious time or my breath in pursuing a matter . . .
Kay Don't talk to me as though I am a public meeting. I said come to the point quick. You're not always so damn long-winded. In fact, you come to the point remarkably quickly at times with the minimum of chat— and we know what times they are.

John This is degenerating into a vulgar brawl and I'm going. (*He goes to pick up his overcoat*)

Kay (*exploding*) You're not going! We'll have a vulgar brawl. (*She rushes across to the window-seat and picks up John's bowler hat then just as quickly moves well away from him*) You'll either stay and have this out or I'll knock hell out of your hat.

John You wouldn't dare. Not my hat!

Kay Just give me the chance. And believe me, I won't just bash it in so that you can knock it out again. I'll rip the brim off your status symbol.

John This is all thoroughly undignified. Give me back my hat.

Kay Why do you wear a bowler hat? Is it a crown of respectability? (*She puts it on her head*)

John (*shouting*) If it was, you could scarcely wear one.

Kay (*shouting*) We're off! (*She takes his hat off her head and slams it on the floor*) Right-ho, my dear, this has been boiling up for a few weeks now.

John makes a move towards his hat

Don't come any nearer or I'll jump on it!

John stops

So I went out to lunch and you're instantly suspicious.

John I have every right to be . . .

Kay You have no rights at all. If you must know I went out to lunch with a friend . . .

John That I can well imagine.

Kay An old school friend.

John Co-educational schools are very popular.

Kay You—you . . . (*With fists upraised in anger she suddenly jumps within an inch or two of the hat*)

John (*shouting*) Don't do that! Be careful!

Kay It was a girl-friend! Girl! And having spent two hours listening to her eulogize on her pimply-faced infants, suffered acute indigestion, and come back to you, you'll be damn lucky if you don't have to buy a new hat when you leave here. The trouble with you . . .

John That's typical of you. Taking a man's hat. You're taking an unfair advantage . . .

Kay Don't interrupt, I haven't finished. You've changed, John Browne, by God you've changed.

John And you're in the process of changing if you haven't changed already.

Kay (*ominously*) I don't think you value this hat after all . . .

John Oh to hell with my hat.

Kay That's the first sensible thing you've said this afternoon. To hell with it! (*She kicks it furiously across the room to John*)

John (*picking it up and wiping it*) You've dented it!

Kay I wish your head had been inside it. When we first met six months ago you were a kind, ordinary, lovable man . . .

John And when we first met, you . . .

Kay (*shouting*) And don't interrupt because you've got your hat back. And either put the bloody thing on your head or on the window-seat, but stop caressing it.

John slams it on his head

John Satisfied? Anything else?

Kay Not much. You've changed, you've changed. You're no longer the John Browne with the funny little "e".

John I've been made well aware of that.

Kay Not by me you haven't. It's you that's changed. (*Suddenly her temper leaves her and she speaks quietly*) I really was attracted to you, and that was the reason I saw you again and again until—well, the inevitable happened. I loved you, because whatever your opinion of me is, bed doesn't come that easy. O.K., so you're married, so we've had an affair. We haven't trod the path of strict virtue, but then we're no different to quite a lot of people. But there was something between us that raised it above the level of plain sex, and it was that something that satisfied your conscience and mine. But you've changed, how you've changed. I'm questioned, you're suspicious, my life is no longer my own. I am possessed in more ways than one. I am your property and you want me like that. (*She holds out her hand and clenches her fist*) You've become a little dictator. (*Her voice gradually rises*) This is your first affair. You've blossomed, you've opened out. You've rediscovered yourself. You're mentally saying, "I too, have a bit on the side." You can really take your place in the club now, you're one of the boys! You're like a damned cockerel strutting around the farmyard, but you're not roosting in my nest any more—so leave the key on your way out! (*She abruptly turns away*)

John (*exploding*) I came here this afternoon . . .

Kay For one reason. Your damned, jealous suspicion. And I'm fed up with it.

John I came the wrong afternoon, no wonder you were surprised to see me.

Kay (*swinging round*) Do you mean to insinuate . . .? (*She moves up to him*)

John I'm not the only one. I've thought for . . .

Kay You—you . . . When you want to hurt you really know how to do it. (*She turns away*)

John It's a pity that you didn't get back earlier.

Kay (*her back to him*) Really!

John You missed your gentleman friend.

Kay My what?

John He said he knew you as well as I do, and from the way he knew this flat I have no reason to doubt him. Who was it—Graham?

Kay How should I know? You saw him. Didn't you exchange cards, you seem to have exchanged everything else.

John He was very discreet, he never left his name.

Kay Then I can't do much about it, can I?

John Oh, but you can! He had the damned impertinence to write a letter to you while I was here. It's in your desk. And believe me, I'm going right now. He's probably waiting across the road, anyway.

Kay goes across to the desk, opens it and takes out the letter, while John furiously pulls on his overcoat. Kay looks at the letter

Kay That friend of mine has left a note as you said, but it happens to be addressed to you.
John What?
Kay Your name is John Browne. He's even spelt it with that stupid little "e".

John comes forward and takes it from her and looks at it in amazement. He looks at Kay and then he tears it open. He reads it, and Kay watches his face. He finishes it and struggles with his emotions. Kay takes the letter from his hand

May I? After all, it was in my desk, written on my paper, and it is from my gentleman friend. (*Kay proceeds to read it out, aloud*) "Dear Mr Browne, or may I call you John? I feel I must write this to you instead of a note to Kay. However, do please tell her to ring me. I assure you it is important, but quite innocuous. I'm afraid I pulled your leg quite considerably this afternoon, I couldn't resist it. You were so damn pompous, and so bloody rude, you deserved it. After all, my dear fellow, it wasn't your flat. But what annoyed me more than anything you made it so apparent that you suspected the worst. I don't object to you thinking that of me, but I strongly object to you thinking it of Kay. It so happens, I'm very fond of her. If you have been foolish enough to tell her of your suspicions before telling her of this note—God help you! I'm afraid, in fact I'm sure, that I've put you in a very awkward position that will need from you the most abject apologies to Kay. You deserve it. I am unrepentant. Do please tell Kay to ring me. Kay's ex-husband, Ian Brent. P.S. By the way, old man, didn't it strike you as odd that whereas I had to ring, you had the privilege of a key?" (*She folds the letter and passes it to John*) Your letter! You must have been very rude and pompous. He has a wicked sense of humour, particularly if he's upset. I do see him sometimes you know. We're still very good friends.
John I'm sorry, I made a mistake. I'm ...
Kay (*turning away*) It's nearly four o'clock—
John Listen, Kay, I'm ...
Kay —and we know how Miss Adams worries. She'll be waiting. Good-bye!

Kay turns and goes into her bedroom

John stands for a moment then screws the letter up and throws it on the floor. He goes to the window-seat and picks up his umbrella and goes to the front door and opens it. He pauses and looks at the closed bedroom door and his glance travels round the room. He goes to go out then stops and slowly moves back to the telephone-table. He takes the key out of his pocket and drops it on the table. Then he moves abruptly to the door

John exits, closing the door

There is a moment's silence, then the telephone begins to ring

A pause, then Kay enters from the bedroom. She has obviously been crying. She glances at the closed front door, pauses a moment, and briefly wipes her eyes, then sits on the couch and lifts the receiver

Hallo! Kensington eight-one-seven-two. . . . Ian! Your sense of humour hasn't improved with time. Thank you for spoiling my afternoon. Why did you do it? . . . I know, I suppose he did seem like that. . . . No, I'm not crying. . . . It doesn't matter. . . . It really wasn't your fault. It was ending anyway. . . . All right, all right. . . . Yes, I *was* crying, for the man I met, for the man *I* met. Not the one you met. . . .

While Kay is listening to Ian's reply—

the Curtain *slowly falls*

FURNITURE AND PROPERTY LIST

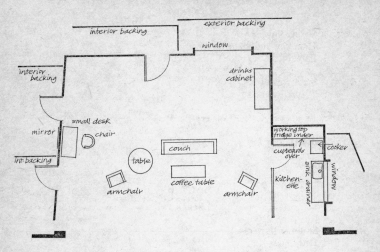

ACT I

SCENE 1

On stage: LOUNGE

Large couch. *On it:* cushions

2 armchairs. *On them:* cushions

Window-seat. *On it:* cushions

Desk chair

Coffee-table. *On it:* ashtray, cigarette-box, lighter, magazines

Occasional table. *On it:* telephone, large vase of spring flowers

Drinks cabinet. *In it:* whisky, gin, sherry, brandy, orangeade, soda-syphon, assorted glasses

Small writing-desk. *In it:* writing-materials, notepaper, envelopes. *Over it:* large mirror

Carpet

Window curtains

KITCHENETTE

Gas cooker. *On it:* whistling-kettle

Sink with practical taps

Draining-board. *On it:* cloths, mop, cleaning materials

Refrigerator. *In it:* milk, dressing

Round walls: cupboards with crockery, sugar, tea (including tin of tea-bags), cake in tin, tin of biscuits, various groceries

Working-top along wall under cupboards. *On it:* trays, cutlery tray, matches, dressing

Off stage: Parcels, new hat in one **(Kay)**
            Parcels **(John)**

Personal: **Kay:** handbag with door key
            John: cigarettes, lighter

Scene 2

Strike: Spring flowers
            Handbag and gloves
            Parcels

Set: Summer flowers
            Tidy kitchenette

Off stage: Basket of bottles **(Delivery Boy)**

Personal: **John:** door key, handkerchief

ACT II
Scene 1

Strike: Summer flowers
            Dirty glasses
            Tea-things

Set: Chrysanthemums in vase
            Tray of used dishes on coffee-table
            Coffee percolator on cooker
            Tray with 2 coffee-cups and saucers, spoons, sugar bowl, cream-jug,
                on working-top
            Newspaper open at crossword, and pencil, on occasional table

Scene 2

Strike: Chrysanthemums
            Coffee tray
            Dirty glasses
            Newspaper and pencil

Off stage: Glass of white liquid—bismuth **(Kay)**

Personal: **John:** umbrella, wallet with driving licence
            Visitor: pen

LIGHTING PLOT

Property fittings required: wall brackets, kitchen ceiling light
Interior. A lounge and kitchenette. The same scene throughout

ACT I, SCENE 1. Afternoon
To open: General effect of bright spring sunlight
No cues

ACT I, SCENE 2. Afternoon
To open: General effect of warm summer sunshine
No cues

ACT II, SCENE 1. Afternoon
To open: General effect of autumnal light
No cues

ACT II, SCENE 2. Afternoon
To open: Room dim with winter dusk
Cue 1   **John** switches on lights   (Page 42)
             Snap on wall brackets to give cosy glow

EFFECTS PLOT

ACT I
SCENE 1

Cue 1	**John:** ". . . into several editions." *Kettle whistles*	(Page 3)
Cue 2	**Kay:** ". . . it was rather nice, too." *Telephone rings*	(Page 12)

SCENE 2

Cue 3	**John** moves towards bedroom door *Doorbell rings*	(Page 26)
Cue 4	**Kay:** ". . . he's not on either." *Kettle whistles*	(Page 30)
Cue 5	**Kay** leads **John** to bedroom *Telephone rings; followed by doorbell*	(Page 33)

ACT II
SCENE 1

No cues

SCENE 2

Cue 6	**John** moves to sit on couch *Doorbell rings—twice*	(Page 42)
Cue 7	After **John** exits *Telephone rings*	(Page 54)

MADE AND PRINTED IN GREAT BRITAIN BY
LATIMER TREND & COMPANY LTD PLYMOUTH
MADE IN ENGLAND